Becoming a Bird

Stephanie Radok is an artist and writer based in Adelaide, South Australia. Her writing was first published in the art magazine *Unreal City*, which she founded with eX de Medici in Canberra in 1986. She has worked as a redoubtable art critic for *Artlink, The Adelaide Review* and other publications. In 2011, 2012 and 2013 she co-edited the first three issues of *Artlink Indigenous* with Daniel Browning. In 2013 her book *An opening: twelve love stories about art* was long-listed for the inaugural Stella Prize for writing by Australian women.

Stephanie Radok's survey exhibition *The Sublingual Museum* was held at Flinders University City Gallery in 2011. Her artwork is held in the National Gallery of Australia, the National Gallery of Victoria, the Flinders University Museum of Art and private collections.

Also by Stephanie Radok

An opening: twelve love stories about art

Julie Blyfield
(with Dick Richards and Julie Blyfield)

Becoming a Bird

untold stories about art

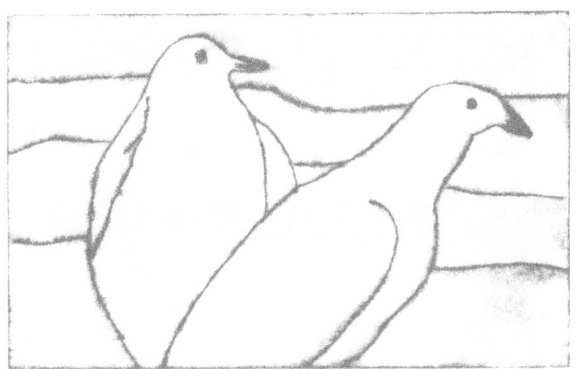

Stephanie Radok

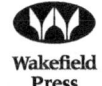

Wakefield Press

Wakefield Press
16 Rose Street
Mile End
South Australia 5031
www.wakefieldpress.com.au

First published 2021

Copyright © Stephanie Radok, 2021

All rights reserved. This book is copyright. Apart from
any fair dealing for the purposes of private study, research,
criticism or review, as permitted under the Copyright Act,
no part may be reproduced without written permission.
Enquiries should be addressed to the publisher.

Edited by Julia Beaven, Wakefield Press
Typeset by Michael Deves, Wakefield Press

Some of Stephanie Radok's travelling was assisted by the
Australian Government through the Australia Council,
its arts funding and advisory body, and by GAGPROJECTS.

ISBN 978 1 74305 802 2

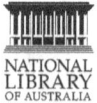
A catalogue record for this book is available from the National Library of Australia

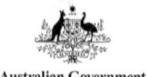

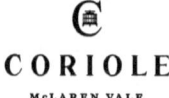
Wakefield Press thanks Coriole Vineyards for continued support

For my parents

Our strategy should be not only to confront empire, but to lay siege to it. To deprive it of oxygen. To shame it. To mock it. With our art, our music, our literature, our stubbornness, our joy, our brilliance, our sheer relentlessness — and our ability to tell our own stories. Stories that are different from the ones we're being brainwashed to believe.

Arundhati Roy

Contents

Introduction		1
JANUARY	*the place of light*	12
FEBRUARY	*the great silence*	19
MARCH	*looking for the foot*	34
APRIL	*the shapes of plants*	49
MAY	*wasting time*	63
JUNE	*getting lost*	74
JULY	*inside books*	86
AUGUST	*finding wildness*	99
SEPTEMBER	*walking it out*	111
OCTOBER	*the quiet dark*	128
NOVEMBER	*the dodo and the dappled garden*	144
DECEMBER	*words for home*	156
References		171
Index		175

Introduction

One day in Venice, rather than rush to see as much as possible of the Biennale of Art (which is spread all over the city as well as grouped in national pavilions in the Giardini) I decided to look inside the San Marco Basilica, the domed and spired building facing the San Marco Square. It is like a fragment of the Byzantine Empire (and indeed includes bits of it) or one of those shiny mirages that often appears in the distance at the end of a road, way off in the sky or across a long open space in Australia.

People were standing on platforms because of the tidal rising water (high water/*acqua alta*) in the Square. The wooden platforms with metal legs were like primary school tables. Part emergency, part musical chairs, part playground, part mystery tour, much dreamlike unreality.

After being in Venice for a while you realise that this mysterious old city is not *on* the sea it is *in* the sea and the sea is a most marvellous pale green mostly. And if you have time to realise it part of you is ready to dissolve into it, to let go. Salt to salt.

I jumped up on a table and joined the queue, not sure exactly where it was going. It was a day for cutting loose rather than being dutiful. It turned out to be going in a simple loop in and out of the vestibule. And you had to be quick and watch your step while looking around so you didn't slip into the water. There were no handrails, just yellow lines painted on the edges of the tables. And the water was inside the vestibule too, a clear rocking salty layer over the beautiful elaborate marble-tiled floor.

But you must look up. The first dome contains amazing mosaics of Genesis stories, in three concentric ascending layers accompanied by Latin text. Here the story of the Creation is told in twenty-six scenes, beginning with the separation of light and darkness and concluding with the expulsion of Adam and Eve from Paradise. The mosaics were made around 700 years ago, and it is said they were composed from the vivid illustrations in a book made in Greece in the 5th century, brought to Venice following the sack of Constantinople in the Fourth Crusade in 1204. The book is now in fragments in the British Museum and is called the *Cotton Genesis*. It is called that odd name because it was last owned by Robert Cotton, a 16th- to 17th-century English antiquarian, parliamentarian and founder of a great library. In 1731 a fire destroyed most of his library, including the *Genesis*, which is now just eighteen scraps of vellum.

One of the reasons I wanted to see the mosaic of the fifth day of Creation, when the birds and fishes were made, was because for many years I have had a laminated colour photocopy of this particular panel stuck to the wall just above the soap holder over my bathtub and I look at it every day when I am at home. Not from the bath but from the toilet. And I am always delighted and charmed by the brilliant energy of the fish and the birds, their presence and their sense of independence. They are ugly, they are beautiful, they are high-spirited and bristling with life just like the birds I see in the garden or the fish I buy to eat.

How did they get into my 1920s pink-terrazzo bathroom? Well, I was doing research for a talk I called *The Immigrant's Garden* for the *Compost* program of Artist's Week during the Adelaide Festival in 1996 and came across the image in a book in the Barr Smith Library and organised a colour photocopy of it. Sitting over the bathroom sink is another picture I had done, a 12th-century fresco from Umbria in which Adam is naming all the creatures in creation. They stand in a dappled garden and are pressed against him in different poses and scales. There are at least four birds not flying but simply standing in the sky while a cow is up a tree angling its head down at him. There is a stag, a snake, a fish (also floating in the sky), a unicorn, a griffin, a sheep, a goat, a pig, a dog and two large geese standing right behind him. He has rather vacant eyes and his right hand stretched out. Clearly that moment of creation was when normal things like gravity were suspended.

Both these images are about creation and creativity as unpredictable, full of possibility, transformation, and metamorphosis as well as wonder and hope.

The narthex – or vestibule – of a Christian church is traditionally the place for penitents or the unconsecrated like me. The mosaic I wanted to see was there and step-by-step I quickly approached and passed it with my fellow travellers. Though made so many years ago it was in glistening good condition, all the gold and blue and white tiles shining.

On seeing the exit loom up quickly (just after a corner with a shop selling postcards and other souvenirs), the table-walkers began to wake from the dream of the mosaics and start stalling or complaining, and shifting their attention to sounds around them. Also coming back to earth and opening my ears, I heard someone say – among American accents asking 'Now when was the Renaissance?' – the critical words: 'I want to see the inside, I think you can go upstairs back here'. I took note and, breaking from the onward flow, turned and avoiding eye contact walked back through the queue slowly and purposefully on the very edge of the tables.

There is a modest door to your right where you enter the vestibule. It is open or closed depending on the time of day and the mood of the workers. It leads to the San Marco Museum. Once through the door you climb a steep and narrow flight of stairs at the top of which you pay a negligible amount. You are now in a small, eccentric and practically empty museum crouched above both San Marco Square and the interior of the Basilica.

Here you are almost alone as few find the door. You can linger and look. You feel like a guerrilla tourist. You do not feel under surveillance at all, although they may be there I saw no cameras. There are many signs asking you to be quiet as it is a sacred space. In fact a sign says in French, English and German: 'SILENCE. Out of respect for this sacred place it is forbidden to give explanations inside the Basilica'. I appreciate this comment on the value of silence.

High up in the building you feel free. In the museum are the *Quadriga*, four great bronze horses stolen from Constantinople, Persian carpets (and you can't help but wonder whether carpets or tiles came first and whether they imitate each other), manuscripts, fragments of earlier mosaics, and here and there odd disconnected almost disinterested educational historical paragraphs. The *Quadriga* went to Paris with Napoleon to sit on top of the Arc de Triomphe for eighteen years before being returned. Their collars cover the breaks made when their heads were removed for travelling.

Up here, no longer in a crowd or an insistently and continually moving queue, you are able to take your time, to linger, to walk outside on the balcony, and quietly stand beside the great bronze horses that are copies of the originals inside. I felt both honoured and surprised at the ease of getting to such an intimate part of this remarkable place, and to be both alone and unsupervised. Restoration was underway on the balcony and thin plywood barriers, metal scaffolding and clamps held things together. The work was propped up with whatever was useful. It was deeply ordinary like home.

From this vantage point on a crowded city constantly moving with tourists you can clearly see the windows and balconies of those who live nearby. You can feel the impatience of the closed windows waiting for your absence, thus gaining a sense of the parallel lives lived around tourist sites. Later I sensed some local political perspectives when I saw *Tourists Go Home, Migrants Welcome!* scrawled on a metal rolldown shop door. And then on a metal rubbish bin near a bridge: STATELESS PERSONS PAVILION.

From my position up in the sky I took photographs of the two nearby sculptures that sit on the top of two pillars looking over the sea. One is the symbol of Venice, a winged lion with its paw on an open book, representing Saint Mark (legendarily the first person to write the story of Jesus), and the other is Saint Theodore of Amasea, the patron of the city before Saint Mark. He holds a spear and stands on what looks like a smallish crocodile (representing the dragon which he was said to have slain).

The winged lion, like the *Quadriga*, was taken to Paris by Napoleon and then returned. It has clearly been added to and repaired many times. It broke into twenty pieces on its return from France, and the different colours of bronze – sea-green, glaucous blue, green-grey – it is made of are clearly visible. Yet when I photographed it with a seagull standing on its head it looked like a joyful crazed dog trying on a pair of wings as much as a lion and, because of a small box or monitor on its platform, as if it was listening to a radio.

It is consoling to look across at this fragmented creature on his pedestal, and see the unfocused white stones of his eyes, his free smile and all his different body parts showing their various colours. He is a model of endurance, of the hybridity of history, the mutability of stories, patched together like a philosophical proof that a lion is still a lion even though most of it has been replaced with parts of other beasts.

When I travel I look for treasure, for old and new ideas and sights, to learn what I cannot learn at home. And I always look for Australia. I was a child living in America when I was told that Australia, where I was born, was the name of the place I came from. As an involuntary exile I needed to discover it for myself. My loyalty is to a place of incredible light, long indigenous histories, the home of my recent ancestors, a place of possibility, of many cultures coming together, where any day something new might be created or something old recreated, a place of great beauty and subtlety, humour and wisdom. It has problems of course but immense potential to solve them. In many ways it is an unknown place globally; many of its stories, memes, experiences beyond stereotypes are invisible, unknown, secret. Above all to me it means a sense of space – living in the sky as much as upon the earth.

And whether I travel or stay home I look out for indigenous people and their cultures. I value their perspectives and philosophies, which constantly assert a familial relationship to the entire non-human world, all the way from animals and birds to hills and rivers. This is more and more important for all of us in terms of learning about different ways of being. For we are all indigenous to the earth and need to look after it in the most thoughtful and careful ways possible. And then I go back to thinking about what the Aboriginal artists at Papunya said to Hossein Valamanesh in 1974 when he asked if he could do a dot painting. 'Yes,' they said, 'but tell your own story.'

Art is often seen as icing on the cake, something to distract people, the spectacle part of bread and circuses. But it is really a place for dissent, analysis, confrontation, celebration, rapture, learning. A place where you can do dangerous things but not be in danger, where you can be controversial and be listened to without fear of reprisal (in some countries anyway), where you can hypothesise, generalise, be specific, light, heavy, oblique, critical, precise, angry, examine the past or the future, go out on a limb and fall off, fail, fail again, stay there, or get up and keep going. Art is continually reinvented and that is why it has so much value. You can't pin it down and tear off its wings. Or if you do they grow back.

When I lived in Canberra I made an artwork, a photocopied collage, an artist's book, called *The Province is Ideal for Art*. I took ponderous sentences from a small cheap paperback book on American art called *The Pocket History of American Painting* by James Thomas Flexner, first published in 1950, and combined them with a postcard image of Pompeii with Mount Vesuvius in the background, scientific diagrams of a frog dissection and images of notable sites taken from a tourist guide to Canberra. Thus juxtaposing art, science, the local and tourism. The work questioned authority and commented on the way art is often discussed – as if there is only one story. Maybe being provincial is ideal.

There is art history, there is art theory, there is art criticism, but there are also much larger stories about art that involve its vital place in our lives, for confrontation, healing, growing, enriching and expanding. There is liberation theology, perhaps too there is liberation art for freedom and justice.

'Don't "we" me!' is one of my favourite shouted phrases when listening to the radio or reading – the assumption that I can be told not only how and what to think but even more patronisingly what I actually do think, as if I am a machine programmed to obey, makes me very bad-tempered indeed. So I write. Because too often art has become institutionalised, thus narrowed, because I am trying to understand myself, because there are too many voices forgotten and too many stories covered up. Because language is life, language is a bell. Because art and culture are too important to everyone to be swallowed up by the marketplace.

Travelling from the South to the North is still to travel from the colony to the empire; the post-colonial to the imperial. It is still to encounter yet again the very credible but often very skewed one-sided (and one-gendered mostly) stories of human culture, of treasure and rescue, of civilisation and discovery, of expansion, of booty, and the arrogance that explains the world from one point of view.

In Australia, as in many other colonised countries, post-colonialism is a lived condition rather than a theory. The post-colonial condition involves a strong awareness of how history has been written, used and discussed. The point of being post-colonial is to *not* see the world in terms of One and Other. It is to escape such simple binaries and certainly not to replace them with more. It is to acknowledge that it is possible to see and describe many histories of the world, and that they interlock and overlock like threads in sewing. Thus recognising a much much richer world of interrelationships than 'them and us', the explorers and the natives, the strangers and the familiars, the centre and the marginal.

And in the idea of travelling in the North, of leaving my province, my region and my village, a plan to encounter important cultural touchstones was upon me, plus a notion of gathering insights, and maybe making statements of great profundity. I put this last desire down at least a bit to the German strand of my heritage, because I know not everyone feels like this. Then again it could be from my Jewish or Irish strands and their storytelling ways.

Birds were around more than 150 million years before humans. It is said that they are a kind of dinosaur. Recently it has been revealed that birdsong began in Australia. We can learn a lot from birds, paying attention to them means hearing a magpie sing in the middle of the night, a kookaburra laughing when you stand in the garden. Being strafed by bright green rainbow lorikeets. The tsk tsk of galahs. The shrieking of sulphur-crested cockatoos. The piercing notes of the piping shrike. The long slow wing flaps and the creaky call of yellow-tailed black cockatoos who once gave me some feathers on Christmas Day.

Becoming a Bird connects stories about travel and home, museums and memory, art and freedom, reverie and nest-building with what is at hand.

Before leaving home to visit many museums in the northern hemisphere I went to Central and to Northern Australia to see some of the really old art of my country.

Throughout Central Australia the light is hugely fragile and clear, and the ground sparkles with soft red earth and mica. This makes every day feel both hallucinatory and super-real. Running east and west of Alice Springs/Mparntwe are the parallel ridges of high mountains called the MacDonnell Ranges. To me these great ramparts of eroded rock look like the ancient ruins of immense buildings. To the Arrernte, the local

Aboriginal people, they are the bodies of caterpillars. Once you know that you start to see them. The names of the caterpillars are Yeperenye, Ntyarlke and Utnerrengatye.

Here and there the caterpillars seem to curve into the earth creating gaps in the ranges. It is said the gaps are where their enemies the stink bugs ripped off the caterpillars' heads. At Emily Gap and Jessie Gap you can see paintings of the caterpillars, the striped lines vertical on the rocks are painted red and white, ochre and lime. To see them is to witness and feel a vibrant link between story and land, hand and eye.

Then I drove out west from Alice to Hermannsburg/Ntaria and saw Albert Namatjira's country, its marvellous blue and pink hills, their eloquent folded powerful shapes against the sky. And in the bush garden where I stayed it seemed as if many of the birds, little honeyeaters especially, were coming to talk to me.

In Northern Australia I drove from Darwin to Kakadu National Park and as I reached the entrance of the Park stopped at a toilet block. Immediately a bird dropped a branch of flowers at my feet. I was alone and this gesture was welcoming and calming. It was only my first encounter of many with the birds living there. It was near the beginning of the dry, in the season of waterlilies, called Yegge by the traditional owners. The intense sense of moisture in the air felt healing and soothing.

I stayed two nights and joined the Yellow Water Cruise on the South Alligator River in both the evening and morning. I saw many birds: crowds of wandering whistling ducks, sea eagles in pairs sitting in trees, lovely bump-headed black-and-white magpie geese sitting awkwardly in and falling out of trees, and the elegant long-toed jacana waterbirds stepping out across waterlily leaves, the chicks hiding under their parents. I went to see the famous delicate rock drawings and paintings at Burrungkuy. It was here something special happened after I had looked at the art and stood nearby quietly thinking and noticing how the trees looked like they had been painted too. In the stillness I heard running water. There was nothing written about it on the information boards and I could not see its source but the gentle musical sound of living water was a secret gift to take with me on my travels.

Yesterday the young magpie who is growing up in our garden found his voice, his warble, his collection of liquid notes, and sang them perched on an arm of the glory vine. Again and again he opened his beak a little and vibrated his singing voice and I, sitting with the dog quiet and still on the sofa watching and listening, thought how he was doing something that came like a gift, like breathing, as well as something that reminded him of his parents and the comfort of being cared for. Afterwards he stretched, first one leg then the other, and his wings. Then flurried his feathers and dug around in his shoulders a bit with his beak.

JANUARY
the place of light

The thing you've got to offer is the thing that started you off in the first place.
                    Rosalie Gascoigne

My earliest memory is uncertain, affected as it is by photographs and stories. I know that I had red hair and a red face when I was born and that sometime in my first year I almost died of some gastric complaint. In an early baby photo I look like I had no hair at all but sit swathed and snuggled down on my mother's lap like a smiling Buddha or a toad with great glowing inward-gazing eyes. My sister looks on. Did the fact that I almost died make me more precious to hold? Perhaps. Another thing I know is that I had no name at all for a while and was simply known as Baby or Bubba.

What I am really trying to think of is my first private or secret memory, which must have been when I was about four and had something to do with keeping a secret – walking barefoot in the creek at the bottom of the street when told not to, getting a splinter, keeping it hidden until it was necessary to confess because of swelling, blood on the socks, pain, a limp, and being taken to the doctor.

JANUARY – the place of light

So stoicism, self-reliance, stubbornness, secrecy were there from the beginning.

It is said I took a long time to tie my shoes and read the time. These things did not seem so important.

Earlier than the splinter was the earthquake in San Francisco. We were pulled by my mother under the big white table with black legs while the world shook, things crashed down and vases toppled. Also in California I recall standing at the backdoor and seeing that slugs had eaten my sister's marigolds in a pot, a kindergarten project. And there are photos showing me taking my very first steps in Golden Gate Park in a tartan skirt stretched over a fat toddler tummy.

A later confidential vivid memory was the complicated nature of friendship, being asked to be the best friend of more than one person and telling each it was her but I would say the other and then not being able to say anything at all. And ending up alone for a while. At around the same time there was the matter of the great dare, licking the pavement. I couldn't do it but remember still looking at someone's wet tongue shape on the grey-brown dusty concrete ground and almost tasting the grit.

What else – being able to read before going to school, being known as a reader and speller, a word person. Liking rhymes and liking words. Memorising poems. Liking books and art. Painting my companion Teddy. Liking the idea of being with Teddy for ever and ever. Asking my mother if my husband would mind if Teddy slept with us. Driving across North America from coast to coast three or four times. Sitting quietly in the backseat. Making up games to pass the time. My defiance about food. Being knocked down by a bicycle in Amsterdam. Having a birthday there and finding my small presents hidden in the hotel room.

Getting up in the middle of the night on Long Island and

watching TV with my mother and being terrified by the film about *The Wandering Eye,* which travelled in a cloud and sent its misty tentacles under the door into a cable car to strangle people while the eye looked on. Having nightmares about the eye.

Refusing to eat fritto misto in Venice and getting no cassata for dessert. Not minding because not liking cassata. Getting lost in Venice, seeing the hotel but only on the other side of a canal. Watching glass being blown. Talking in my sleep and saying, 'What time is it in New York?'

Looking out of the window of my bedroom of our two-storey house on Long Island and seeing my father fall down a ladder and into some bushes. Then there was the hula-hoop we threw into the large pine tree next to the house and the rare uncle who climbed up to get it down. Uncles were rare because we rarely saw them. Another time we met an uncle somewhere in Europe who took us to a toyshop and said choose anything you want. A startling experience. When we moved to Adelaide another uncle lifted me up to see the peach blossom.

These are tiny scattered fragments of stories, some mine, some family folklore, little dogears of memory that don't mean much but mark time as if it was an old book.

In the beginning we lived in the bush. The world was light and shadow, green and brown, yellow and red, blue and white. The borders of the house that my parents built in 1953, in Ringwood in Victoria, were square but open to the sky and trees on all sides. And flung up into the sky to be on a level with treetops. Being in the bush and the slim endlessly sliding shadows of the gumtrees on the walls of the house like a painting are what I remember most clearly of this place.

JANUARY – the place of light

As we left there when I was only a year old this vivid memory is assisted, if not invented, by a very short film made in 1954 by my aunt Gundula, my father's sister. The Kodachrome film is of the house as much as the family. It shows my father walking down the stairs that wind around the house with my sister on his shoulders. Our dog Winky is there too, and a neighbour's child. My mother and I are sitting on the steps at the bottom. In a pale-blue jacket I am hugged onto her like a koala. Everyone in the film does the awkward self-conscious thing of standing in front of the camera as if hypnotised by it.

The film emphasises that the house was located not near but nestled right in the bush. It was made of wood and perched on a slope with its L-shaped balcony up in the air among the slender gumtrees. It had a wide white chimney. One of the most insistent parts of the film shows the swaying tree shadows on the chimney as hypnotic, constant, elusive. And trees can be seen beyond the top of the chimney as well.

Propped against the windows on the ground floor are sloping panels of framed glass squares. I am sure they were placed there by my father and that they imitated something he knew in the northern hemisphere, like cold frames, a way of protecting what is planted underneath. As well as being lattices for climbing plants.

That house at Oliver Street is gone now and Ringwood is no longer on the outskirts of Melbourne. Anyone who has ever looked inside the front of a Penguin knows that for many years Ringwood was the home of Penguin Books in Australia; it is also the place where the famous Pride of Ringwood hops were developed for Carlton & United Breweries. In the early 1950s Ringwood was mostly bush. Here young families, many of them immigrants and refugees, Italians and Balts, bought bush blocks and helped each other on weekends to build their first homes.

An old black-and-white photograph shows a cement mixer surrounded by proud couples and vegetable gardens.

The end of the film shows the inside of the house where my parents sit at a table with Gundula's husband, my uncle Jim, all drinking coffee, talking and smoking. My red-headed mother smiles at the camera directly then hugs me. I am sitting on her lap and call importantly for something. My father is seen to understand what I am asking for, passes my stuffed dog to me and all is well.

The last few seconds of the film cut to the sparse living room where we children are quietly playing on a big red carpet while my mother reads a book. On a rudimentary wall shelf behind her are arranged a few vases and two boomerangs. I still have one of them. It was given to my father on 10 July 1950 when he stopped working at the Aeronautical Research Laboratory at Fishermans Bend. Among the sixty or so signatures in black ink is that of his own father, Fritz Radok, for whom he had found a job at the Laboratory as a cleaner.

Also on the shelf was propped a print of a Renaissance painting, *Portrait of a Lady* by Giovanni Ambrogio de Predis. It is one of those paintings showing the profile of a pale face on a dark background staring from right to left that has a very strong air of duration, almost like early photographs where people's heads were propped up for the exposure. It includes a sense of the eyes of the artist walking slowly over the skin of the sitter like an ant. De Predis is said to have worked on Leonardo da Vinci's *Madonna of the Rocks*. This painting is as familiar to me as the face of my mother or father: the soft curve of the neck, the delicate reddish hair held down by black ribbons, the orange top over which a cream yoke is stretched across her shoulders, a sense of waiting and attentiveness. It sits nearby as I write these words. On the back a label says that it was printed in

JANUARY – the place of light

Amsterdam in 1930 for the Rijksmuseum so it may well have once belonged to my grandparents.

I also have a small black-and-white photograph of a corner of that room in our house. It shows two sets of French doors and three windows. It was a very light-filled place. The simplicity and bareness of the room is touching. Under the windows are three layers of bookshelves not especially tidily crammed with books. This feels very familiar and much like a legacy, perhaps the truest legacy of this small family. Read and you will find richness, places to stay, to hide, to occupy, to long for and to love.

There is a rug on the wooden floor and on the rug is a simple wooden child's rocker with a penguin transfer on it. On the window ledge above the bookshelf is arranged a row of barely visible tiny animals that I just know are there. At one end there is a much bigger deer made from wood with a very strong grain. That deer turned up recently. It was sitting quietly on a shelf somewhere waiting to be recognised and is on my desk now. I think my parents must have got it in Europe. Perhaps it was a present from someone for my sister who was born in England in 1952.

The deer has a northern hemisphere flavour of a piece of folk art made by someone who has made many such animals, but the eyes are completely wrong. They are in the wrong place, are cut roughly and are not both the same. Really the deer needs no eyes any more than it needs a nose or cloven hooves. It is, after all, a wooden animal. I wonder if a child complained about the lack of eyes and they were added later. Or the child cut them so the deer could see. I'm starting to think it was me.

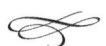

In the early morning I walk in the garden around the edges of the known world. I observe each tree, shrub and plant and their relation to each other, their health and happiness. The dog accompanies me and does his own thing, walking extremely slowly under overhanging jasmine or fennel fronds and letting them trail over his back, or throwing himself upside down in the sun, all four legs in the air like a dead wombat, or intensively chasing a skink through rocks and weeds.

FEBRUARY
the great silence

She could listen; she was like a room of vases: you enter and find your sense of yourself sharpened by a vague, tranquil expectance in the air.

John Updike

Somewhere in my shed/studio is an old wooden box that originally belonged to the schoolfriend of a boyfriend of mine. It is lined with frayed faded blue silky fabric, has a curved metal hook to close it and a small brass keyhole with no key. I never met him but his name is written on the top of the box in pencil. He was a butterfly collector and it was his butterfly box. When I received it as a gift from my boyfriend (or did I claim it?) there were pins, loose wings and small flat paper bodies in it, discards from this devoted amateur scientific work. The wings were still vividly coloured, in particular I was delighted by a few tattered Ulysses butterfly wings in that incredible heart-expanding iridescent blue that is backed by a dull grey-brown.

I kept the box as it was, looking into it occasionally to enjoy the wings and to reflect on the patience and dedication required to locate and collect butterflies, kill them, identify, classify, conserve and pin them. Then one day I decided to tip out the old things and use the box to store brushes and tools wrapped in an old piece of suede. Then the box got covered up by other tasks and objects and left alone for a long time. When I got back to it one of the brushes I had left in it, a very fat Chinese one with a bamboo handle, was a mere skeleton – or rather the brush end of it was, having been eaten away by some creature. As I began to empty the box once again I noticed a small roundish insect rushing around inside it and realised that it was someone's home, a really large one, complete with butterfly fragments, suede wallpaper, Chinese bamboo and goat hair. An elaborate palace for a small being.

Since then every time I try to clean or move things in my garden or house I am newly aware that I am in someone's else home, that indeed homes are everywhere; in summer if I move the folded beach umbrella a spotted gecko will be revealed, if I shift an old wooden box more geckos will be disturbed, if I lift a stone, fat pale worms as thick as my little finger, thin pink ones, masses of pleated grey slaters and shiny black beetles will need to move from where they are living. Spiders watch me every time I pick up a broom, and there are certain regular birds – magpies, crested pigeons, turtledoves, rosellas, rainbow lorikeets, noisy miners – taking over the yard (whose yard?) and at least two possums sleeping in tetchy solitude in the roof at least some of the time. When it rains snails are dancing or sailing along the paths and I must watch where I walk.

Though occasionally alarming or annoying my co-existence with all this wildlife makes me feel rich and happy, and often in a state of wonder and surprise at all the energy constantly coexisting beside me. Apprehensive about changing anything, yet always looking for a clear space to breathe.

Sometimes, in this house that contains so much stuff from four generations and a bit, and so many objects, each with a story and a history, I become aware of myself as a little like

FEBRUARY – the great silence

that bug in the old butterfly box, pottering around arranging iridescent fragments of blue wing, goat hair and bamboo from China. As insignificant, as private as a bug in a box, as busy as calm as quiet as contented as sleepy and dreamy in a seemingly permanent suburban world laid down in South Australia not very long ago, less than a couple of hundred years, between the hills and the sea.

From the street you can see the shining flaring white edge of the sea to the west; and to the east, unless the clouds disguise them, you can see the hills. If you walk a bit you can see the tips of the TV transmission towers, the scars left by quarries and sometimes smoke from burning off or bushfires. And up there is Mount Lofty with its lighthouse-like obelisk, and there is one particular hill with a pure circular arc, a purple-red ground and distinct tree silhouettes spiking out of it.

In this suburb in a room in a house in a garden in a book on a shelf behind a door in a cupboard, complete worlds are present and folded together. And make up an intellectual history as well as a tale of the senses, a story of both contemplation and action. It seems that this house, any house really, is also a museum.

And perhaps the garden is a museum too, a place crowded with history and provenances and places to hide, with metaphors and stories hidden in the soil, held in leaves and flowers, in colours, scents, petals, stems, roots and branches. The briefness of flowers, the incredible growth of fruit, the patience of plants, their stillness and forbearance, their quiet imperceptible development. Though they co-exist with us their sense of time, their lives, are so different. Yet we are companions.

How do you define a museum? As a place of safety, of knowledge and learning, of excess that can both make us small and expand us. A place where the past is definitively ordered even though the majority of the many objects that outlast people are stored out of sight. A place then of taxonomies, categorising and gatekeeping, selecting and ordering. There are rules, fashions and objects, and there is the past, piled around our ankles like leaves.

Reflecting on the origins of museums there is the story of the *Wunderkammer*, literally 'the wonder room', the cabinet of curiosities, the collections of objects that often a rich person begins, obsessively overdoes then gives to the state either because the family is not interested, for tax reasons, or because of their desire to share the wonders of their hoard. The power of an individual, of the state, of empire, of a country are held in museums which try to tell – and often, it seems, to possess – the story of the entire world in their language, from their perspective. Thus their apparent implicit ownership and possession of the world, something they try to share in being open to visitors.

In such a place, cultural, natural and legendary items are placed side by side – unicorn's horns, paintings, mermaid's tails, pieces of the true cross, turtle shells, seedpods, insects, minerals, crystals, totem poles, weapons, boats and crocodiles, rare plants, stuffed birds and animals, maps, books, words and artefacts from all over the world. They are crowded together indiscriminately or with exotic dioramas, suggesting that while this is everything there is always more. Infinite riches. And knowledge is what is possessed but also excess to need, beyond counting or comprehension, and hence something that can never be owned.

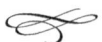

You enter the Pitt Rivers Museum in Oxford through the Oxford Museum of Natural History. It has the flavour of a cabinet of curiosities: it is dark (they lend you a torch as soon as you enter) and it is very crowded, with boats suspended in the air, three great totem poles from Canada, and masses of vitrines stuffed full of objects from all over the world. In this museum stuff is arranged not by chronology or country or importance but by function. The categories are marvellous in themselves – whistles, drums, magic, treatment of the dead, writing and communication, smoking and stimulants, methods of making fire, textiles, dwellings, coiled baskets, rope and string, lamps and lighting, pottery, drums, ivory, bone and horn, trumpets, amulets and charms, flutes, games, surgical instruments ...

The Museum was founded in 1884 when archaeologist–anthropologist Lieutenant-General Augustus Henry Lane Fox Pitt Rivers gave his collection of 22,000 collected, bought or traded objects to the University of Oxford. Since then they have gathered or been given another 200,000 and are still collecting. Significantly Pitt Rivers was especially interested in weapons and made charts for his lectures showing typologies and chronologies with a particular evolutionary approach to human artefacts, for example they show his idea of how a straight stick evolved into a spear while a curved one became a boomerang.

As a museum the Pitt Rivers is a real time warp, a time capsule, an actual slice of a past way of thinking and ordering human culture. When I visited I saw the Joint Head of Collections Jeremy Coote, who told me they are redoing the cases to make them still seem 19th century but getting more and more material and information into them, thus subtly deepening, enriching and updating the collection. So that like many other museums it becomes an artificial time zone in some ways. Falseness and make-believe is a certain part of museums, even as they seem to deal in truths. Next time you stroke a meteor at a museum have a close look at its label, chances are it is a cast or replica.

Re-making museums in a post-colonial world has a lot to do with re-viewing the world, re-examining its division into the West and the Rest, and the placement of indigenous and 'foreign' peoples into natural history or 'other' status – or not. Yet in spite of all that genuine questioning museums often still maintain a stance of a certain 'we' overlooking, describing and explaining the world. Doesn't that ethnographic anthropological gaze need to be turned onto everyone?

One of the design experiments conducted by the team working on the controversial Humboldt Forum, the massive new museum to display Asian, African, American and Oceanic collections in Berlin, did just that. There was a series of tall vitrines arranged in the entry hall of the soon-to-be vacated Ethnographic Museum in Dahlem. Visitors were encouraged to leave their possessions in them as they would in the cloakroom. The glass boxes had keys like any locker but they immediately put your possessions on show as if you were the subject of a museum display.

Where do museum collections come from, how were they collected, where do they belong? Are the histories of their collection of equal importance as the items? Should objects be returned? Do they reinforce stories of colonisation and empire – how can they confront them? These questions are often asked by museum professionals and percolate out more or less clearly. Artists and writers also ask.

Children start to make their own museums when they collect and arrange objects on a shoebox lid, on a shelf or in a drawer. And that early personal relationship to objects, the handling, arrangement and display of things with stories, with provenances and relationships to each other, is surely at the heart of any museum. Objects are juxtaposed with each other and communicate snippets of stories that enfold time, memory, emotion in their colours and forms. And thus preserve some kind of private intimate space, which engenders a dreaming state, a trance that encompasses the deep past and the present. And it need not be about possession or ownership but can be internal, involving the deep corridors of the imagination.

The first museum is often said to be Plato's library at his Academy, north-west of the centre of Athens in an olive grove sacred to Athena, goddess of wisdom (though the grove also has connections to the god Prometheus who stole fire and put it in a fennel stalk to give to humans, and is named after the Athenian hero Academus who saved Athens from destruction by the twins Castor and Pollux). This mingling of myth and reality gives the story life.

I once played Athena in a school play because the teacher thought I looked ethereal. Peaky, my mother called it. She was always grabbing me and trying to paint roses on my cheeks with lipstick. We did the story of Arachne, who claimed to be the best weaver in the world, thus pitting herself against Athena. Humans always come off badly in such encounters. After the contest Arachne was turned into a spider. This is why spiders are called arachnids.

As Athena I wore a toga made of metallic purple fabric woven from thin copper thread and a thin stiff cotton. It smelled of metal — a bitter dry scent. All of us in the play wore garments made from this scratchy fabric in different colours — purple, pink, green, gold — equal parts metal and cloth. The wardrobe area located under the wooden stage at the school contained an extraordinary collection of ancient garments, some probably recycled from the early days of South Australian colonisation, some made by keen creative mothers. In particular I recall trying on an elaborate winged unbleached calico dress with rough red oxide lines painted on it. Perhaps it was a costume for Ariel.

Who has not been a flower, a fish, a fairy or an elf at some stage in their life? I remember being the sun, the moon, a star; it was a kindergarten thing that was over too quickly. Like imagining being a growing seed experiencing rain. This particular slow seed was just beginning to stir, to awaken, to feel the air, to consider what it meant to come to life when the rest of the group was onto the next thing – being lions, kangaroos, teapots or birds.

I remember another occasion when I was a tree, this time wearing brown tights and a green skivvy with leaves sewn on it. Real leaves being fragile, these leaves were made of paper, cut and painted. What about the head, the bark, the nest of a bird, fruit, and so on? We never got that far. And once my son had a paper crown with leaves standing straight up, stapled to it like ears, a wreath-necklace of red and blue-green eucalypt leaves, and armlets of bark. The very simplicity of the costume, its unlikeness, allowed space for transformation if not transfiguration.

Olive trees are said to be the oldest cultivated trees in existence and can live for thousands of years. There are olive groves throughout the parklands that ring the city of Adelaide, most of which were planted in the early 1870s. But the history of the olive in South Australia began in 1844, just up the hill from where I live, at the village of Beaumont, now a suburb.

Samuel Davenport, who lived at Beaumont House, introduced the trees and encouraged others to grow them as a source of oil. He imported the first trees from Sicily in 1844. Only seven years later, the Great Exhibition of the Works of Industry of All Nations in London at the Crystal Palace included a bottle of olive oil from South Australia said to be of exceptional clarity, colour and flavour.

Thousands of olive trees were planted on the Stonyfell foothills, 120 acres, 10,000 trees. Many of the olive trees planted in those days have a strong dignified and graceful presence today, their trunks are now thick, grey and gnarled, you often see them by the side of the road or stumble upon them lined up in groves, or individually in the suburbs, in the foothills, and in the parklands. Once you start to notice them you tend to see them everywhere. It is hard to believe that none of them are more than 200 years old.

They are also present in noxious weed proportions as feral trees planted by birds, running away along the creek beds and gullies through the hills. And in gardens as either treasured or ignored individuals. Oil presses were also brought in and at a park in Beaumont a large granite one once used as a wine press in Chile can be found. The Adelaide Gaol had the first commercial olive press in Australia. Those olives were harvested by 'lunatics' from the asylums, and by destitute women and orphans.

Just a few photographs remain of the artwork placed in an olive grove in the East Park Lands by Hossein Valamanesh for the 1980 Adelaide Festival. Called *Dwelling* it was a very simple adobe Middle Eastern-style house with one door, two latticed windows, a fireplace and a wooden ladder to its roof.

It was designed by Valamanesh and constructed by him with members of the Roundspace artists' co-operative. It stayed there for eight months. The initially reluctant local council grew to like it and wished it could stay but it was not built to be permanent. I didn't see it but I really like its ephemeral nature, its simplicity and literal earthiness, and the photograph of it in which you can see how it is both foreign and fitting into its location in the olive grove.

Olive trees are clearly not native to Australia, though like eucalypts and many other Australian trees they are not deciduous, have dull-green and silvery leaves and fit in very well to the tones of the bush. In South Australia, often said to have a Mediterranean climate, the olives have 'gone native' or become naturalised. So although they are accidental invasive weeds they are also deliberately widely grown for oil, and for their fruit.

The Aramaic word for oil press is Gethsemane, the name of the garden at the foot of the Mount of Olives in Jerusalem where Jesus spent the night before his death. It was a place he often went, making it easy for his betrayer Judas to find him. Because of this tragic role the word Gethsemane necessarily possesses a historical and religious weight of sorrow, as well as its own rhythmic beauty. 'Oil press' just doesn't have the same ring – though has some implication of suffering.

The Mount of Olives in Jerusalem has been a Jewish cemetery for many centuries. In photographs it is white with gravestones. It is said to be where Jesus ascended to heaven and where, when the Jewish Messiah comes, the resurrection of the dead will begin. Hence the cemetery.

In spite of the fact that olive trees can be feral pests there is something about them that is very attractive. The olive branch is a symbol of peace in Jewish, Christian and Arab traditions. Olive trees evoke abundance, purity and quiet power, tranquility and order. They suggest places where each year the same seasonal rituals are carried out, where fruit is collected and oil is pressed, where jars of olives and of oil are stored, where an expectation of ongoing peace, prosperity and above all good simple self-sufficient eating is possible even though their sites of origin – Syria, Greece, Turkey, Italy – have often been places of conflict. In Palestine they represent resistance and resilience.

Maybe any group of trees, or even just one tree, orchard or not, is a sign of order, of sacredness, of the way things can be structured, and respected. A tree is a world. Holding up more than half the sky. When you plant a tree you are starting something. And it is a great feeling when that tree is old enough to stand firm without moving when you shake its trunk. The more you notice trees the more you feel their presence. A few of the red gum trees that I see while walking are so big they must be many hundreds of years old.

Glynburn Road rises sharply at Beaumont. Here, in the backyard of the house where one of my school friends once lived, are evenly spaced olive trees, the remnants of the huge orchard that reappears like a Mediterranean ghost throughout the suburb. I remember as a child giving each tree the name of a country and running from one to another as bases. Making up stories was the basis of our play. I was considered to have an imagination, and we would roll down the hill, be saved and lost in storms and floods, fight pirates and see whales, become ill and die, be brought back to life, talk to animals, be captured, bound hand and foot and escape, see dragons and unicorns, ponder peace and war, tell secrets and find refuge, hospitals, ships and forts in these trees. They were easy to climb and each tree had a different character or mood. Yet there was a family resemblance to them because they were the same species and part of a grove that placed a structure on the land.

The olive plantation, painted in 1946 by South Australian artist Dorrit Black, memorialises the olive plantations of the Adelaide foothills by showing the regular patterning the trees made. In the painting the curves of the hills are a lot like shoulders and the land is like a body but the trees are almost machine-like, striping the hills with order. The olive groves are no longer maintained as they were when Black 'took' the painting, but you can still drive straight out of the city up Norwood Parade until it becomes Coach Road, look south and see where she looked across the hills.

Black spent her childhood just up the road from me in a building now demolished though some of the trees still living there, Aleppo pines in particular, echo the strong full forms characteristic of her paintings and prints.

In the 1920s Black engaged with Cubism in Paris, and in 1931 she established the Modern Art Centre in Sydney, the first gallery in Australia to show modernist art. Though adventurous in her work, she was drawn by her sense of duty and obligation to respond to the needs of her family, who also supported her financially. She spent her last twenty years away from big cities living in Adelaide where, after nursing her mother for five years, she finally, at forty-eight, achieved a purpose-built studio-home of her own at 14 Romalo Avenue, Magill. In 1951 when she was sixty, Black died from fatal injuries received in a car accident four blocks from where I live. In 1946 she declared: 'It is the artist's business to reveal to mankind a new outlook on life and the world.'

A less well-known museum origin story is set in the Mesopotamian city of Ur and features a woman called Ennigaldi, the daughter of the last Neo-Babylonian king, as the first museum curator. Her collection of assorted artefacts had what are considered the first museum labels – on clay tablets in three languages.

My favourite museum origin story comes from Pausanias, a traveller, geographer and writer from ancient Greek times, whose stories once thought to be wholly imaginary are often found to be quite accurate. For example Heinrich Schliemann, the 19th century archaeologist of the nine layers of the city of Troy (which was itself once thought to be a fabrication, a fiction

FEBRUARY – the great silence

made up by the blind Greek poet Homer rather than a real place), followed Pausanias' accounts to locate the site of Troy.

In his chief surviving work, *Description of Greece*, Pausanias wrote about what he observed as he travelled, whether large or small, old or new, ordinary or legendary. Among other things he describes visiting the grave of Orpheus, whose lyre-playing and singing could divert rivers, and charm all living things and even stones.

Pausanias suggests that the word 'museum' originated as the name of a small hill in Athens opposite the Acropolis. The hill was called Mouseion after Mousaious, a man who used to sing on the hill, died of old age and was buried there.

There is something irresistible for me about this story because I have an obsession with hills. Also because it links singing, ageing and death. And if you think about museums as places where things go not to die but to be cared for, and where their voices (perhaps singing) are kept together, there is some joy in thinking of Mouseion as the place where museums began – it leaves space for more unpredictability and creativity in the manifestations of museums. When we sing or become lyrical we lift off. Can our voices be kept? Songs in a museum?

This obsession with hills – what is that? Well, hills. They are hypnotic. You can look at them from a distance, be surrounded by them or walk upon them. Light describes shapes on them. They suggest that something greater lies beneath them, that the earth is a body. When you look from a distance, a hill appears still, it could almost be painted on the sky. Activity on that hill, such as animals, plants, wind and so on, is as busy as elsewhere but the blueness of distance creates the illusion of stillness, a stillness that can lead you to feel that the hill is watching you, or has a secret life, or is removed from this world and is partly in another one. It is an intimation of eternity that is sometimes also present in art. If we could just hold life as still as that hill we might be able to understand it, to unfold and examine it.

And I am thinking of particular Australian hills that I know. It is almost as if they are a form of writing you must learn to read, and the sense of a message is there most profoundly. It is an internally felt message of contrast, of darkness against light, force against force, softness against softness, longing against distance. The song of the earth in some way.

In one of the many large books I have on Papunya Tula art, *Papunya: a Place made after the Story* by Geoffrey Bardon and James Bardon, there is a photograph by Allan Scott of two men standing looking at the camera, behind them are two hills, the Honey Ant Hills – Warumpi and Tjupi – that clearly hold a story or two. The caption says *Dancing possum story 1973* and the men's names, Tim Leura Tjapaltjarri and Old Henry Tjugadi Tjungurrayi. The men have tall headdresses topped with emu feather tassels, their faces and bodies are decorated with paint and tufts of brown-and-white fluff, each holds a stick and great bunches of gum leaves are tied to their legs. They could be brothers, the hills and the men. And possibly are. The photograph shows the approach of the evening, the sky is pink and fading behind the hills and the caption says that a number of men got ready to be filmed but the light went too soon. This photograph holds so much, bearing witness to a dance that didn't happen and the time and place of its making.

At times it has seemed to me the clearest and simplest thing to know is that all art and culture ought to be about where you are, that the stories you tell and the art you make need to at least attempt to be mostly about your surroundings, your own byways and highways, and not be leaning on those of other places.

But sometimes you forget and wonder why you aren't in Berlin.

FEBRUARY – the great silence

The dog and I walk twice a day, morning and afternoon. As we cross the oval we are often circled by swooping swallows as our walking stirs up small insects for them to catch.

For our early walk we often go to the fenced playground at the top of the street with a tennis ball. With a fresh eager face he runs for it but never brings it back. When a jogger goes past he runs very fast next to the fence and barks at them.

He likes to check the unfenced park nearby where someone throws old bread and occasionally an old roast lamb bone over their fence. Here the Aleppo pines are ravaged by the yellow-tailed black cockatoos who tear open the cones for pine nuts.

When we are in these parks it sometimes feels as if time has stopped and we will always be there – suspended between the trees that look like candlesticks in the sky.

MARCH
looking for the foot

To be an artist, you need to exist in a world of silence.
Louise Bourgeois

At a dinner at Henley Beach one evening the artist Derek Kreckler told me about a room in the Pergamon Museum in Berlin that contains just one enormous foot. I never found it when I went there but the idea of it was a dream drawing me on, a vision, something to walk towards, something to imagine – inching around the walls of a huge gallery circumnavigating a giant foot like the one that crashes down on the opening credits of Monty Python.

It is a strange fact that the Python foot is not some cartoonist's whim but is based on the Foot of Cupid from the 16th century Florentine painter Agnolo Bronzino's painting *Venus, Cupid, Folly and Time*. Cupid is bending over his mother Venus, squeezing her breast and kissing her lips while his right foot hovers over a pink-beaked white pigeon whose head is flanked by the head of another pigeon facing the other way. You often see birds sit or stand together like this – it is a way of keeping watch. They seem to be sleeping but if you are watching closely, you will see a wrinkled eye open from time to time.

I am very fond of my postcard of Bronzino's 1545 painting

of Giovanni de Medici as a child. This work stood out among the endless rooms of paintings in the Uffizi in Florence as radiating love, which was what I had decided to look for in order to survive the experience. Maybe I was suffering from Stendhal syndrome brought on by seeing too much art. The image reminds me of my son when he was small. It shows a chubby-faced child in a deep-pink costume glowing with a smile and holding a small bird to his chest.

A giant foot in a museum would need to have been lowered in by a huge crane, or have the gallery built around it. It would need a ship to itself. Or a specially built truck. It would make you think about scale and ambition, and vast civilisations crumbled into dust, about immensity and nothingness. And about the ambition and covetousness and purpose of transporting a giant foot from Greece to Germany. Taking responsibility for world civilisation no less. Messianic or Napoleonic though it is, it does appeal to me.

When I was a child and thought about such things I imagined the foot of God. As no one has ever seen him he is invisible. He is standing on the earth and always watching you, from a distance. He is so big you would only ever encounter one of his feet, much like the foot in Monty Python. And as it is invisible you could walk into it again and again, like repeating a stupid mistake, but there would never be anything there. And the other one would be miles away.

Out of the blue I was asked to stay in Berlin at Phasmid Studios for two months. It meant a return to solitude such as I had not experienced since I was a graduate student in Canberra in the late seventies. And it reminded me of the ANU campus with its residences and lawns, flat 1940s buildings and deciduous trees. What is this fond dream of being an artist and writer in residence? In my case it involved intense isolation and a challenging level of confrontation with the self.

In a way it meant entering into a kind of psychoanalysis, self-observation, travelling back through your life ... not because you want to but because it happens when you are isolated. Thinking of friends and incidents long-buried, starting with the negative ones and hopefully working through to the better. And somewhere is the belief that you will become more healthy and more who you are meant to be. That in fact painting and drawing might make you well and perhaps writing too. Art as catharsis and healing.

One thing I noticed was that I was always looking, communing with what was around me, closely observing trees and fences, buildings and light posts as if they had a message for me.

I remembered that as a child I used to often find things on the ground – money, insects, jewellery. So in Berlin I regularly dropped copper coins near the children's crèche to help them learn to look.

I also remembered that I could wiggle my ears. We used to watch and squeal with laughter when my father did this. The issue here is to locate the relevant muscles and twitch them. I am strongest with the left ear, whatever that means.

I remembered that one possible career I had imagined as a child was to be a window-dresser, arranging things in clean well-lighted places. And I thought about food a lot.

Maybe a residency is a holiday – where you treat yourself with kindness. And there are displacement activities. Like sweeping and drinking. I swept the floor. Why was the dust so dark grey? And where did it come from? Did its colour have anything to do with the smoking chimneys dotted around the city? What were they doing?

MARCH – looking for the foot

On this land to the east of Berlin near Marzahn there were once gypsies, Russian soldiers, animals at market. Now new houses imitating old houses are being built. Neat and bare, with nothing around them to hide in they seem vulnerable and intensely provisional. The wind, the wolf, will blow them over, these toy houses with vulnerable gardens and thin walls.

Opposite the Studios was a parade ground with towering 1960s four-headed light poles sprouting out of it. The lines on the ground receded to a low hill of refuse covered in weeds, pointing and stretching, falling and dying. Behind the hill was a row of trees, birches, surrounding another light pole. And a very large chimney.

Waste land or wasteland, what is the difference? I was told this land is clean in terms of poisons, explaining the many weeds and birds. A family of foxes lived in the bush on the sides of the nearby railway line. Every day many large black and grey crows patrolled the ground. And once I saw wild ducks flying from the west to the east and two herons.

From the studio the line of trees against the low grey sky looked a bit like an Anselm Kiefer painting – romantic and apocalyptic, suggesting the upheavals, cruelty and devastation of history as well as the regrowth, the weeds that spring out of it. His work is sentimental, narrative and picturesque yet elemental and draws me in to want to touch it. At Phasmid in the early dark of a northern winter I brought weeds inside to paint and covered the windows with my paintings.

I never found the foot in the Pergamon Museum and still wonder if there is a gallery there that I missed. A secret space that only a few people find, that lurks as a dream gallery or lost courtyard that is talked about but rarely seen. I never sat down to cross off all the rooms I visited over several trips. Instead I was lucky enough to have time to wander, note and photograph.

I was familiar with a staged photograph by Thomas Struth of the Pergamon Altar in the Pergamon Museum with people stiffly arranged around it. Struth was a student of the Düsseldorf artists Bernd and Hilla Becher who, over many years, relentlessly photographed water towers and other structures of industrial architecture with close and archaeological eyes. They began in 1959 by photographing the industrial constructions connected to the steel and mining industries in the Ruhr Valley in Germany.

The photographs show that these *Anonymous Sculptures*, as they titled their first book, are monumental and eloquent. An archaeology of the recent present, of technology, they show the significance of these structures as designs and as objects, and at the same time they list them endlessly like items in a catalogue or encyclopaedia of plants or animals. Like flowers or insects, hills or lakes, the industrial architecture is revealed as almost endless variations on a theme. And even though they seem objective somehow there is emotion embedded in them. It is the passion for the code, the archive, the collection.

The works recorded the changing face of German industrial architecture as both design and environment for an uncaring present and an unknown future. They collect a history that may easily have been unrecorded, as indeed so many unspectacular and ordinary histories are. I think of the sprawling idiosyncratic low-slung houses with great character that are being demolished every day in the suburbs around me in Adelaide. I am certain that no one is recording them before they vanish forever, replaced by ugly big square box-like houses with no verandas, no charm and no real gardens. Their faces are turned inwards to large illuminated screens. Their backs are smooth concrete and they have steel barred gates like prisons. Part of me wants to write all over them. Building houses without verandas in this climate doesn't make sense. How can people imagine their lives without verandas?

In his book *Veranda: Embracing Place* architectural writer Philip Drew noted:

> *The vacancy of the veranda is both an invitation and a challenge: an invitation to fill it with life and a challenge to see that the life which it shelters has real meaning ... from the veranda, former Europeans confront a landscape which is a great reservoir of spirit ...*

The Bechers were pioneers in teaching photography at the Art Academy in Düsseldorf in 1976 when painting was considered the most important art form. I first saw their photographs at the 1979 *Sydney Biennale: European Dialogue* curated by Nick Waterlow, in a satellite exhibition at the Australian Centre for Photography. I recognised something tough, mesmerising and haunting about them, their decisiveness, and conviction, their relentlessness and strange detached aura of implausible beauty.

One of the Becher's students, Thomas Struth, made his reputation through photographs of urban streetscapes and posed family portraits. His photographs are often so large they engulf the viewer. In 1989 he began a series called *Museum Photographs* showing the interiors of famous museums. From 1996 to 2001 he photographed inside the Pergamon Museum, the first time he made a series of photos of just one museum.

First he tried taking an image of the 2nd century BC Pergamon Altar, with the museum's daily visitors arrayed on its steps and around the room. Then he decided to stage a photo and pose people. A lot of Struth's museum photographs look much like those any visitor takes, with their inevitable random depictions of other visitors also taking photos, or talking on the phone or to each other. In Struth's series in the Prado in Spain and the Hermitage in St Petersburg, which are without staged posers, the people mostly seem more interested in each other than in the famous paintings. Admittedly many are schoolchildren.

Those random moments of the lives of others (who we never noticed at the time) are like short stories or fables when we later see them trapped in our photos. The many facets of that couple's relationship, the pondering evil eyes, the vacant stares, the person who seems to be examining us with distaste or anger as we inadvertently incorporate them in our images, the sleepy one, the repressed boredom in that child, the shirt on that man, the joy in that woman.

In Struth's staged Pergamon works, all that human weirdness and idiosyncracy, just about everything really, is replaced by slightly self-conscious student types, mostly in dark clothes, posing as tourists. They seem about to break into a tutorial. This has the effect of emphasising our habitual self-consciousness in front of Great Works of Civilisation; the material culture held in museums and which it seems we must digest, assimilate and live up to or be forever Uncivilised. And yet somehow there is a story in Struth's images that is like the Becher's portraits of water towers. The photographs put the people on display as much as the Altar. The story is about recording daily life in a museum, the voracious worldwide consumption of remnants of human history that seeks the freshness and veracity of first-hand experience even as the thousandth person for the day sighs *aah* in the Blue Mosque in Istanbul, or drags themselves towards Botticelli's *Primavera* in the Uffizi.

Then there is the work of Candida Höfer, another student of

the Bechers. Her very large and eloquent photographs are of the grand spaces of museums and libraries, opera houses and palaces all over the world, always empty. Höfer's initial series was of guest workers in Germany. Like Struth she started with people and ended with buildings.

Höfer took a memorable photograph of Nefertiti in her glass box in her special circular room in the Neues Museum in Berlin. The Neues (the New One) was built on Museum Island in 1855, bombed in WWII, left in a ragged state in East Berlin behind the Iron Curtain before being rejuvenated in the 21st century in a unified Germany keen to be a leader in the preservation, display and analysis of world culture. In 2007 when I attended the Basel Art Fair I collected a small free notebook of projects by David Chipperfield Architects. On the cover was their latest project, the Folkwang Museum in Essen, but what appealed to me was another project represented by two mesmerising images of the empty interior of the Neues Museum, one showing a series of fragile painted pillars supported by metal collars at the doors of the galleries receding concentrically into the distance. The seeming infinitude of such galleries is what makes them echo thought.

The other image showed a small section of damaged wall with a chalky blue-and-white diamond tile pattern painted on it; parts of the design were missing, parts were very worn. For some reason the textures and colours especially fascinated me, the abraded surfaces speaking of time, war, memory and the confrontation between decay and structure.

The Egyptian section of the Neues was designed to imitate an idea of Egypt with countless wall paintings and ceiling frescoes. From 1997 to 2009 Chipperfield rebuilt and restored it, retaining as much as possible of its original design as well as bullet holes and other signs of war. Thus the building is like a living thing, its history visible. And it is on what you might call an Egyptian scale with vast sightlines from floor to floor, immense staircases and multiple vitrines full of the residue of the past.

The single Egyptian Room of the South Australian Museum designed in 1939 is Adelaide's equivalent of such a place, though no bullet holes that I know of are scarring its sandstone walls. This room is an amazing time capsule with painted walls that include a striking image of Nut, the goddess of the sky, doing a star-filled yoga pose over the earth. It also holds such treasures as mummified cats and the sarcophagus and mummy of Renpit-Nefert acquired in Cairo in 1890. Every schoolchild that grows up in Adelaide knows that this place is hidden in the heart of the city.

On North Terrace, in the museum's building of many ghosts and lost times (which include the great cases of stuffed animals standing in murky shadows; the glass-boxed glassy-eyed lion, whose tail twitches every three or so minutes; the great Pacific collection of shrunken heads, canoes, masks and other vestiges of island cultures; and the wing holding a display of some of the vast Aboriginal culture collections spanning the country), the Egyptian Room is a specially haunted place. You enter from a spiral staircase inside one of the sandstone towers of the Museum. These stairs are the kind of detail that enters your dreams; I have often climbed them in my sleep talking to various acquaintances along the way.

In 2003 my artwork, *The Weight of Words*, was shown in the Pacific Cultures Gallery in old wooden vitrines, the glass panels of which reflected the decorated canoes hanging above them. I cast twelve books in plaster each labelled with its title and author as a seminal text of exploration or anthropology, such as George Grey's *Journals of Two Expeditions of Discovery* and Charles

Darwin's *On the Origin of Species by Means of Natural Selection or the Preservation of Favoured Races in the Struggle for Life*. Also included were *Native Tribes of Central Australia* by Baldwin Spencer and F.J. Gillen, Marcel Mauss' *The Gift*, James Frazer's *The Golden Bough*, Bronislaw Malinowski's *Argonauts of the Western Pacific* and Sigmund Freud's *Totem and Taboo*. It is a story in which Australian Aboriginal people and ideas about them figure in a large way, even though some of the writers never met them.

The books were white but lightly tinted, they could never be opened. They drew attention to all the cultures without writing and all the words not published, all the silences, all the secrets, all the gaps in knowledge, the withheld and the unspoken. Yet *The Weight of Words* also referred to the weight given to the words that have been published. An information panel ethnographed the books by describing them as sacred objects once kept in libraries but that could be borrowed for four weeks at a time.

What do I love about Candida Höfer's photograph of Nefertiti (whose name means the beautiful one has come)? It is not that I think she is beautiful. Her size in this impressive circular room shows that a resonant object does not need to be large. It is where she is, the worn surfaces, the patchy green and red walls, the damaged but restored floor suggesting past lives, the partly restored, partly painted coffered ceiling, the glass vitrine creating a space within the space. A sense of clear calm space. And a sense of structure set against and among decay. Maybe it reminds me of home where nothing is perfect, where the freedom of imperfection is so familiar and Nefertiti is like a member of the family, an old aunt or grandmother holding her head high, gracious and majestic like Frida Kahlo. And a small Nefertiti did once have a presence on the corner of my mother's old Danish teak desk where I sit to write.

Back to the Pergamon. What are we looking at when we stare

at part of an old Greek temple inside a museum in Germany? Importing the western side of an ancient altar from Greece to Germany is ambitious. Its scale approaches the giant foot idea. Placing an altar that was built outside on the top of a windy hill inside a specially designed building is very impressive. It is a little like putting a tree or a mountain indoors. Is this what museums do best – tame the world?

The Pergamon Altar is quite steep. You are allowed to walk up the steps, and you are allowed to sit on them. This physical interaction with something ancient in a museum is extremely unusual. Really there should also be some continuous feast of food and drink going on up there, or the opportunity to perform a ritual such as making a libation, offering flowers or burning incense to extend the moment.

The event of being there could then be even more interactive, not digitally but as a real experience, of worship or ritual, or reverence ... or maybe a surveillance camera could film each of us ascending the steps then play it back opposite the altar in an infinite series. Something like the heartbeats in *Pulse Room/ Almacén de Corazonadas* by Rafael Lozano-Hemmer, an edition of which is installed at MONA, the Museum of Old and New Art, in Hobart. When you enter you hold metal handgrips and thereby add the rhythm of your pulse to the artwork in the form of flashing light bulbs, rows of which stretch around the room. Thus taking what is inside you and placing it outside. And joining the pulses of those who came before and those who come after you.

But the Pergamon Altar is not in Berlin for religious reasons – but rather historic and cultural ones and, inescapably, reasons of power. The Pergamon Museum was built to house the Pergamon Altar, which was excavated in the late 19th century by German archaeologist Carl Humann. It is said that the

MARCH – looking for the foot

Turkish government is trying to get it back from the German government, though the German story is that it was taken with permission and that the site was being looted for building materials. Would it even exist in its current form if it hadn't been taken away, reconstructed and conserved? There is little chance that it will ever go back to Turkey. In fact the Pergamon Altar Gallery is currently closed for years of renovations, a new glass ceiling and climate control so I was lucky to see it at all. Will people still be allowed to sit on it when it reopens?

In Turkey it is possible to visit the site of the ancient city of Pergamon, eight hours from Istanbul, and see the ruins of this Greek city built 200 years before Christ was born. The modern city of Bergama is nearby. Galen, the father of early Greek medicine, was born in Pergamon. The gladiators he cared for enjoyed impressive survival rates for the time. He called their wounds 'windows into the body'. Pergamon was also known for having a terrific library of 200,000 volumes that Mark Antony stole to give to Cleopatra, and which inspired Alexander the Great to start his library in Constantinople, or so the story goes.

My own personal Pergamon Altar story involves dropping my cloakroom token there, twice, and having to find it. Once I dropped it high up on the Altar stairs and once behind. In each case I broke out in a sweat but actually found it quite easily, that little piece of plastic with my entire life invisibly attached to it. I realised my hands must have opened unconsciously to let it go, twice. What did that mean?

There is an implacable whiteness about the Pergamon Altar, something like that of the Parthenon sculptures in the British Museum. It is vaguely irritating and all too reminiscent of the neo-classical fascist architecture and art that these examples of Greek civilisation inspired. Somehow a false ideal of purity, of technical excellence, of cold perfection comes through, repulsive in its rationality, and false in its whiteness. Yes, yes, it's well-done but somewhat soulless and you can't help wondering why, if the Ancient Greeks painted their buildings and sculpture in bright colours, no museum ever does in its reconstructions? Something is missing here – the contrast of the energy of colour with the relentless firmness of the carving. It looks like the past is being sanitised, made germ-free, safe, cool, white and authoritarian.

It is true that most museums reconstruct many of their exhibits, especially buildings, from fragments rather than simply displaying them as great piles of rubble, which would be a more accurate and telling way to represent much of the past. Or indeed the present. And here and there in my travels through the world's museums I have seen a large nose, a fold, a pleat, a chin or the tip of a huge finger lying on the floor. And immediately look for a wall panel to find out what is going on. They are pieces of a sculpture called *We the People* by Danh Võ, which he had fabricated in Shanghai. It consists of 400 repouseé copper fragments replicating exactly the form and method of manufacture of the Statue of Liberty. 'We the People' are the first three words of the preamble to the US Constitution. The artist has stated he doesn't want to explain the work but it seems to be something about the shattering of an ideal and, I suppose, the scattering of an idea.

But the Pergamon Altar is not the best bit in the Pergamon Museum. The best Big Thing is the magnificent Gate of Ishtar built by Nebuchadnezzar, the eighth gate into the city of Babylon, one of the Seven Wonders of the World. Covered with shiny glazed yellow and lapis lazuli blue bricks and tiles, on which lions, bulls (aurochs) and dragons walk next to flowers and geometric motifs, the giant gate is part of a reconstruction of a path through the city where citizens walked, victorious armies paraded and celebrations occurred.

There are other bits of it in Istanbul, Paris, London and a few other places but the biggest and most spectacular is in Berlin. And this is only the smaller of two gates they have, the larger one being in storage.

The fact that this great big construction is so old and so bright, so beautiful and so alive, and made from brightly coloured bricks, makes the past seem simple and accessible. Like the Doge's Palace in Venice, part of which possesses a pattern formed not by elaborate crafts of surface decoration or painting but by the different colours of bricks, it is easily connected with the scale of the human hand.

Of course the past is not so simple and not so accessible but maintains an emotional charge and relevance to the ongoing history of the region. In Berlin in 2010 Michael Rakowitz constructed an Ishtar Gate from food packaging originating in Iraq. Its title *The Invisible Enemy Should Not Exist*, uses the words that the path through the gate was historically called. It has also been translated as *May The Arrogant Not Prevail*. One of his ongoing projects is making copies of the many artefacts looted from the National Museum in Baghdad in 2003, again from the bright lettered packaging of dates and date products. Their ingenious construction from what he calls the 'material of marginality' make them like toys, like ghosts, like uncomfortable bookmarks drawing together violence, nostalgia, exile and history. A recent work by Michael Rakowitz installed in London on the fourth plinth in Trafalgar Square, made from 10,500 flattened tins of date syrup, is a *lamassu*, a winged bull with a human face, like the massive Assyrian ones destroyed at the historic Negal gate of Nineveh by Islamic State in 2015.

An abridged excerpt of the inscription by King Nebuchadnezzar II on the side of the Ishtar Gate in Berlin says:

> *I (Nebuchadnezzar) laid the foundation of the gates down to the ground water level and had them built out of pure blue stone. Upon the walls in the inner room of the gate are bulls and dragons and thus I magnificently adorned them with luxurious splendour for all mankind to behold in awe.*

Which shows he didn't mind calling bricks stones. Or did everyone have to pretend that the blue-glazed bricks were solid lapis lazuli?

The new dog is the same breed as the old dog but has a very different personality. The old dog was a licker; the new dog only very occasionally makes a delicate almost erotic tasting of your hand with his tongue. He loves to sit or lie very close and spoon up to my body. The great warmth coming from him feels both relaxing and healing. His fur always smells good. Up in Aurukun on Cape York there is said to be a creation place not just for the local ones but for all the world's dogs.

APRIL
the shapes of plants

When you do something exactly wrong, you always turn up something.
Andy Warhol

One of the postcards propped up on the windowsill of my office shows a painting made with oil paint on vellum in 1493 by Albrecht Dürer when he was twenty-two. It is one of his three famous self-portrait paintings, one made at twenty-two, one at twenty-six, one at twenty-eight. After that, as far as we know, he let it go. Each of the portraits are often said to be trailblazers in showing an artist looking deeply and curiously at themselves and thus showing the artist, in some societies anyway, moving away from being a craftsperson, a person doing a skilled job, to a person thinking about being a person as well as showing their pride at the exuberant exercise of their skills.

Dürer in particular was very involved with the depiction of hair. He works it most fully in his last self-portrait where he has elbow-length curly hair and 'imitates' the man of sorrows, Jesus Christ, who surely never looked as directly and intensely at an artist. Yet the idea of looking into someone's soul is especially present in a self-portrait. And when looking at Dürer's intense self-appraisal, as he looked at himself reversed in a mirror, you can feel that you know what it was like for him to look at himself.

In the 1493 self-portrait held in the collection of the Louvre in Paris, *Selbstbildnis mit Eryngium* (*Self-portrait with thistle*) *(autoportrait au chardon)*, Dürer holds a purplish glaucous spiky thistle, a weed. An influential interpretation of the work, said to be by the writer Goethe, is that the painting was an engagement present for Dürer's fiancée. The thistle *Eryngium amethystinum* (amethyst eryngium) held by the artist is called '*Mannstreu*' in German, which also means husband's fidelity or married fidelity. Perhaps the prickliness of it suggests something about marriage. It is also said to relate to Christ – its thorniness connecting it to the crown of thorns and the idea of suffering. Dürer wasn't engaged when he painted it – but of course being twenty-two he would have known an arranged marriage was on the cards. He was in his *Wanderjahre* (wandering years) travelling to learn more skills and see a wider world, which an artisan did between his first training and settling down to establish his own workshop (you had to be married to open a workshop).

From a species with a family of about two hundred and thirty, the amethyst eryngium is regarded as an aphrodisiac. This cosmopolitan weed found all over the world, with its centre of diversity in South America, is also known as amethyst sea holly, or blue devil. *Erynginum ovinum* is a version endemic to Australia. It grew as a weed on Stoney Creek, the property situated along the road to Captains Flat in New South Wales, where I once shared a sprawling group house set on a low hill above a creek. 'Person wanted to share house in country with seven others' was what the ad said in *Canberra Times*. I was working in Canberra as a research officer with the Australian Council for Overseas Aid while living alone in a granny flat, and getting tired of eating the same meal for five days after I had

APRIL – the shapes of plants

cooked a reasonable quantity. So I called and they said come out for lunch on Saturday when *The Goon Show* is on.

There was a gate you had to open and close when you drove into or out of the property. On it hung a wooden sign carved with the words Stoney Creek. Springing out of the pale grey dusty hard earth along the winding road to the house amongst the small tussocks of straw-coloured grasses were these extraordinarily delicate blue-purple spiky thistles. I often carefully collected them and placed them in vases, just to look at their fineness. They seemed too delicate to draw, though I would give it a go now. Noticing them in the self-portrait by Dürer is as strange as recognising my pale northern hemisphere skin in his.

A common definition of a weed is that it is a plant out of place, the implication being that everything belongs somewhere, that weeds too have ancestral homes. Or is a weed simply a plant that is unwanted? All weeds are not the same. Some are feral, destructive and massively invasive. Others are benign, or useful traditional healers. It must have been very early in human life on earth that it became clear that plants were medicine as well as food, either or both, tonic and poison, able to heal and destroy.

The dichotomy of native and introduced plants, and thus a division into belonging and not belonging, falls apart somewhat with the cosmopolitan plants. They were certainly around when the world was not divided into countries or nations, a time well before people. In the beginning was the world, not the word. The words came with the people. An artwork of mine, titled *in the beginning was the world*, consists of layers of brush writing and brush paintings of plant body parts, all of which seem to be balanced in the space above the paper so that neither the words nor the images dominate, neither receding nor projecting.

In some cases the words blur into the shapes. It is literally a demonstration of an equivalence between language and visible things, which does not privilege one or the other but shows them co-existing. It's painted in yellow and red like flames.

Each line of the writing transcribes words from botanic descriptions of the plants as well as the names of the places where they can be found and repeats them like incantations. My chief resource for this work was a small book published in 1909 by J.M. Black, the uncle of Dorrit Black. Coming to South Australia from Scotland in 1877 and working at first as a journalist he botanised all over the state to compile the four volumes of *The Flora of South Australia*. It was his first book, *The Naturalised Flora of South Australia*, with his own line drawings that I was especially drawn to in the beginning because we say that people are naturalised when they become Australian citizens, and it seemed that some parallels could be drawn between the movements and settlements of people and plants. This relates to notions of purity, of belonging, of migration and adaptability. It's a small book with a rough green cover that you can carry in your pocket.

In researching common local weeds in South Australia I found some plants used traditionally in both the northern and southern hemispheres for food and medicine. Thus they showed that rather than the world being divided between the West and the rest, or West and East, or even North and South, it really is One Big Cosmopolitan Place. What does this mean? Maybe only that we all have more in common than we sometimes think we do. That we are all native to the earth and belong to it. Is this too obvious a remark? Can people ever get to a point of seeing each other as they are, as equal beings on the earth? Tasmanian artist Julie Gough told me that a Cherokee man, Thomas Alcoze, told her at an Indigenous Fire Symposium in

APRIL – the shapes of plants

Hobart in 2000 that we are all indigenous but only some of us know where from.

Some tentative early artworks I made when I lived in Broulee, a small coastal town on the South Coast of New South Wales, were pencil drawings of collections of local plants I gathered on my walks with my best friend Maud, the Staffordshire Terrier. In some way the drawings were asserting the importance of looking at what surrounds you, knowing where you are rather than being a stranger to it because you are thinking about being somewhere else where life is really happening.

There is not just one but many ways to make a drawing. An instinctive method is contour drawing in which you draw the outline, the edges of something – its contours – rather than its insides. If well-done the volume of the object or subject is implied. So a curved line on a piece of paper can describe something that looks as if it can be held, or is heavy, has volume and swells out, or even subtly seems to inflect the colour of the paper, creating an inside and an outside, a positive and a negative space. Such a drawing does not try to be a photograph but asserts its handmadeness and its direct connection to thought.

And every drawing is a self-portrait, even of a moment. This is what makes it valuable, like a seismograph of a human interior. And what makes a good drawing is mutable. Sometimes, even often, 'bad' drawings are better and say more than 'good' drawings. Many children's drawings have a purity about them that sets to one side the idea of good and bad and simply speaks of freshness of vision and direct communication.

At that time I really wanted to draw but had to force myself to sit still and stick at it, just to stay in one place is always an effort. My drawing was stiff, awkward and unfluent – yet followed the movement and characteristic shape of each plant carefully, almost as if I was tracing them. When you think about drawing you realise that it is your eye that is touching the edges of what you are seeing and then translating that touch to your hand's movements. That is why after you have drawn something it is newly familiar and almost inside you the next time you look at it.

Tightness, looseness, ripeness, rawness, tradition, innovation, evocation, suggestion, thinking, overthinking, not thinking – all these factors are involved. They burst, they recede. Some artists have a fixed style, sometimes it becomes a formula and whatever they do follows it. Drawing can be alive and exciting, dull and tiresome or in-between.

But how to begin to subvert the long tradition of botanical drawing? By writing with a stick? I tried that in a series of works called *weedmaps*, which showed a plant by itself with writing describing its history and qualities. But rather than beautiful calligraphy the writing was scratchy, uneven, and made with a bamboo pen that had to be dipped often into the brown ink that I used. It deliberately made it hard to read; it slowed down your looking.

The echoes in botanical drawings of other times and places are very strong. Herbals were among the first books produced in ancient Egypt, China, India and Europe. Their significance was in showing images of plants that could be recognised over time and across geographical and language barriers. Yet often the most delightful early images are so stylised and simple that it is hard to see how they could be useful. I imagine that samples of dried or living plants might have accompanied them. So the scent of the herbs would be there as well.

The raw simplicity of early herbals draws together the desires to communicate, to inform, to teach, to decorate and to celebrate. Single medicinal herbs, and the remedies made from them, were called 'simples' in contrast to complex herbal remedies, which consisted of mixtures of herbs.

APRIL – the shapes of plants

Collecting simples, collecting herbs and knowing what to do with them, something that anyone can still do today all over the world, means having a primary relationship with the earth. It is precious and exciting. It means going outside the commercial grid and learning what feel like secrets. When the herbs are weeds growing everywhere for free it is even better.

In China in 1406 an early herbal *Jiuhuang bencao* by Ming Dynasty prince Zhu Xiao was published sixty-nine years before the first European one. It was a guide to famine foods. This is something else I began thinking about when looking at local weeds. The somewhat apocalyptic times in which we live in the early 21st century made me think that all this nutritional and medicinal information about the common plants that surround us could and should be known by everyone. Just in case.

My own interest in herbs goes back to an early attraction to the tranquillity of plants, the pleasure of cooking and reading books by herbalist Dorothy Hall, whose mixture of knowledge, common sense and down-to-earth humour has often led me from dark places to light ones.

While in Broulee I had two books about being at home in Australia that I treasured: *The Penguin Book of the Bush* (1977) by Edward Kynaston and *Wild Food in Australia* (1976) by A.B. and J.W. Cribb. On its cover Kynaston's book has a coloured drawing by Michael Leunig of a man sauntering in the bush. The friendly face of the Leunig character shows it to be a place of warmth and lightness. Birds and marsupials look benignly on the scene. The drawing presents a comfortable sense of home, a benevolent bush. It's a long way from the idea of 'weird melancholy' described by Marcus Clarke that Australians have sometimes been told they believe in. *Wild Food in Australia* was a serious approach to eating off the land. It included some introduced species and many references to Aboriginal people's practices of gathering, treating and consuming various foods. And many pictures of plants that I could identify growing around me, thus fostering the idea of living off and knowing the land you live on, the place where you are. It inspired me to collect and draw local plants.

In Broulee we lived in a beaten-up pink weatherboard house situated in a grove of whistling casuarina trees on the thin winding road through the tiny coastal settlement. The back of the house faced the low dunes behind a headland facing an island. You walked out the back door and straight up a sandhill. Then you could go left through low bushes down a sandy path to the open bay of a small beach or turn right and walk along a trail past the backs of houses, through a narrow passage of bushes and over a low fence onto a road leading down to the long thundering beach stretching all the way to the estuary at Moruya Heads.

Or you could walk up to the headland. The top of the Broulee headland was covered in casuarinas creating a dim and quiet place where their needle-like leaves lay in deep thick soft brown piles. This small forest could be circumnavigated or quietly walked through depending on your mood. The headland looked out to an island. On the long beach from time to time the local Aboriginal people set out nets for fish. Only they were allowed to use nets. A few times I bought some fish from them.

Our friend Blue was a diver and would appear at our house before dawn to take us fishing, or rather to get us to drive him somewhere to go fishing. Later sitting on the sea in a small boat as the sun came up he would offer us cans of beer. Fishing is not necessarily about fishing but about being where the fish live. Sometimes Blue brought us lots of abalone to cook with lots of garlic and once our kitchen floor was covered with live crayfish flapping around backwards on the ancient cracked green lino.

APRIL – the shapes of plants

The back screen door, which banged quite loudly, had a weight on a string to close it. It led into the kitchen, which ran along the back of the house, and had an old wood stove as well as an old electric one, a steel sink in the corner surrounded by windows, cupboards, an old dresser and an eating nook. The front room was a flimsy filled-in sleep-out. The windows between it and the main lounge room had black-and-white transparent photographs of scenic views sandwiched in them, like the ones you used to see in train carriages. A bay window in the lounge room had stained-glass windows. There was one large bedroom with louvred pebbled-glass windows on two sides. A sliding window from the kitchen went straight into another small bedroom. The bathroom/laundry was around the side of the house and the toilet, which was a thickly painted wooden shelf with a hole in it over a big pit, was housed in a little shed up a concrete path on the sandhill behind the house.

The house belonged to a man called 'Old Mick' who lived in Sydney and occasionally came and stayed. The rent was cheap because of this arrangement. There was a locked shed stuffed full of his things which he would look at when he was down. Once he showed us an ancient unopened can of beer. He would train in a blue singlet to run in City to Surf races in Sydney.

A lot of the local people we knew were hippies/back-to-the-earth people living in the Araluen Valley. Some were Rajneesh people dressed in orange, red and yellow living communally further down the coast in the mountains at a commune called Trafalmadore because of Kurt Vonnegut, building their houses from stone or wood or ferro-cement, growing vegetables and marijuana, having children, playing music and eating magic mushrooms. Those on the dole were said to belong to the Sunshine Club.

Mushrooms are a risky business but their effect is often to fill the unconfident with confidence, which can be pretty good. We brought cowpats home from the Deua River flats for my organic garden in the lee of the sandhills and for a while had magic mushrooms growing alongside beans, tomatoes and pumpkins in the backyard. Collecting them in the wild had a dream-like quality. You went out after rain into the bush, parked the car, crossed the river and then wandered through the trees looking. Once you saw one you tended to see lots and lots more of the shimmering tiny golden peaks on the ground. You ate them with pieces of orange or mandarin to hide the taste.

Once you are sensitised to weeds you start to see them and their stories everywhere. A familiarity with their shapes is established that means that wherever you go in the world you not only see buildings or views, shops or streets or monuments – man-made things – but also what feel like close acquaintances calmly living by the side of the road, at the base of a tree or in a crack in the ground on a busy street. When I took a bus from Heathrow airport to Oxford, after flying a day and a night from Australia, I immediately saw from its window large numbers of familiar weeds growing by the side of the freeway waving their prickly, spiky, implacable arms at me like friends. And felt at home.

In Berlin at the Museum für Gegenwart (Museum for Contemporary Art), sited in the Hamburger Bahnhof, a neoclassical former major railway station built in 1846 (where the plum cake at the café is especially good), I found with great pleasure a permanent site-specific artwork by John Knight called *The Right to be Lazy*, which began in 2007 as an idea, and was bought and installed by the Museum in 2009.

Basically the artwork is what grows on the rondel, that circle of ground at the front of the museum, if you do nothing to it. I recognised several weeds and indeed the glorious weediness of it immediately. Its rough overgrown look had the lovely effect of making it appear as if the museum was closed, let go to seed, or otherwise put out to pasture. That sense of desolation, of neglect, made me smile. *The Right to be Lazy* is unusual as an artwork in not jumping up and down and poking you in the eye, in fact probably most people don't even notice it at all. It looks like wasteland, like land left alone, or wild. A careless affront to over-regulation, to any regulation. It is true of course that there are lots of such weedy wild places all over Berlin, walking around you get a distinct sense that the city only has a temporary purchase on the land.

The Right to be Lazy involves a formal agreement between the institution and the artist that the rondel is never to be tended but left to grow with some very basic maintenance. The wildness of the artwork, full of lively recognisable weeds to those who are observant, is in stark contrast to its surrounding institutionalised border of twelve neatly trimmed buttons of hedge.

There is an information sign beside this weedfest on which, beneath the artist's name and the title of the work, are the words: *'Let us be lazy in everything, except in loving and drinking, except in being lazy.' Gotthold Ephraim Lessing.*

Lessing was an 18th-century German writer, art critic and philosopher with strong convictions about truth as something that is never owned but can be approached by anyone; and which must involve the freedom to make up your own mind. The sign also says: 'John Knight's work is named after the influential book *The Right To Be Lazy* (1883) authored by Karl Marx's son-in-law Paul Lafargue who criticised the liberal, the conservative and even the socialist working ethics.'

Lafargue's book is a manifesto in which he argues that only in laziness can ideas come and culture exist. Therefore he pleaded for the three-hour working day and that the worker has a right to his/her own culture. It's revolutionary. He wrote:

> *If, uprooting from its heart the vice which dominates it and degrades its nature, the working class were to arise in its terrible strength, not to demand the Rights of Man, which are but the rights of capitalist exploitation, not to demand the Right to Work which is but the right to misery, but to forge a brazen law forbidding any man to work more than three hours a day, the earth, the old earth, trembling with joy would feel a new universe leaping within her.*

And weeds here represent the freedom to be. Wild. Free. Uninstitutionalised. Deinstitutionalised. Unemployed. And Lazy.

Some accounts of the lives of traditional Aboriginal people in Australia report three hours a day working as an average so maybe they had the measure of this approach a long time ago.

For me there is in Knight's weedy and free work an echo of Dürer's ink and watercolour work *The Great Piece of Turf (Das große Rasenstück)* from 1500, which shows weeds and medicinal plants including my old familiars – dandelions, plantain and yarrow – growing together in a chaotic clump as if spaded up and plonked on the drawing table. It is a drawing depicting a piece of nothing, something kicked at in passing, something you might see by the side of the road or next to a ditch almost anywhere in the world. And the drawing, in showing something very ordinary as splendid, is a corrective to notions of luxury being something requiring the suffering of others.

Another great and memorable artwork using weeds was made by Chinese artist Song Dong for the five-yearly contemporary art exhibition *documenta* in Kassel, Germany, in 2012. It consisted of three man-made hills covered in weeds and was called *Doing Nothing Garden*. A deliriously weedy space, it instantly echoed the dreamy sky-hills of Chinese landscape painting. It was set in the middle distance of the large lawn in front of the huge old Orangerie palace. The lawn edges into a large park with a canal, lakes, forests and various follies to get lost in.

Doing Nothing was written in free-standing yellow neon Chinese characters pegged into the ground of the hills which were alive and crowded with great swathes of some weeds shooting up and going to seed while others flowered, and still others just looked prickly or half-dead. The intransigency of weeds and their frequent ethereal sparseness are among their strong recurring features. With its hills built out of waste and rubble Song's garden was begun in 2010 to develop its established wasted look for the exhibition. The oval concrete edge of the garden was a brown-red smooth lip that could be sat on, and which had the effect of making the three hills echo a scholar's rock on its wooden tray or a bonsai landscape in its container.

Among the many weed artworks that I have made over the years are weed wallpaper, weed paintings on beer coasters, chalk drawings of weeds as immigrant plants and weeds painted on vinyl records as immigrant songs. One of my weed artworks executed just after my mother's death in January 2002 involved placing three wire rings upon three swept circles of ground, and waiting to see what grew. Down the south coast of South Australia in summer inside a pine forest surrounded by vineyards the answer is practically nothing.

It took about ten years of walking in this neighbourhood before the dog and I saw a kangaroo. We were in Ferguson Park at the top of our street, a piece of bush which while it has never been built upon does have naturalised plants from other countries growing in it. We walked up the pale grey hardened dirt path and there in the bushes about to hop away was a large grey kangaroo. It must have come down from the hills. It seemed like a miracle. Its fur was very much the same colour as the earth.

Around the same time at Chambers Gully off Waterfall Gully Road we saw a large male grey kangaroo. He was standing on a flat piece of land halfway down a hill where once a house must have been built as an old tank is nearby. There was no doubt that he saw us though he didn't move away. I firmly distracted the dog. A distinct communication passed between us as I looked into his eyes and slowly moved away. I said something to him though I can't remember exactly what, something polite, respectful and pretty thrilled.

MAY

wasting time

Art is intimacy, lover's talk, and yet it is a public declaration.
Jeanette Winterson

I sit on the front veranda after gardening and listen to the wind. When I close my eyes all the colours in front of me become a sheet of glowing pink as the sun shoots across my vision. The dog who is normally lying down and wondering why I am always so busy is intensely worrying at a bone, grinding it, bouncing its gristle, cracking the very hardness of it with his jaw. I wish I had his focus and concentration. Later he will snore deeply, passing out in an easy chair but always able to spring up in a moment and follow me wherever I go.

But at this moment it is I who am still, with my legs draped over the cane table, holding the stillness, this peace, the quiet in my eyes, my skin and my thoughts. An old friend comes to mind, he is smiling and being delightful. What a wonderful surprise.

I have some need to explore where I am and where I have been and to ponder angles and perspectives. Going to friends' houses as a child I often insisted on walking around the outside of the house exploring the site, the garden, the rooms, the look of the place from different directions and angles. Some friends who had grown up in those houses and lived in them their whole lives had never been all the way around the outside. It was their first time walking along with me.

The domestic sphere, so often considered a woman's place, is full of stories that have not been told as often as those of battles and mappings of continents, yet it is clear they are as full of war and journeys. The struggle to create a life, to maintain it, to shape and hold and then eventually let go of it is mostly as private as it is unspoken.

To build a garden, to let it develop, to feel its sense of eternity and to accept its temporary nature. To see the house as a museum to live in, the garden as a sanctuary to circumnavigate, the views from each window as paintings holding enough to reflect upon for a hundred years or more. And to see how the domestic is connected with art and ideas, with culture, and to see how they always have been connected. To think about being European and Australian, Asian and African, Aboriginal and original, in other words to be human, to join the past and the present, to link books and reading with breathing and watching birds and looking out for insects and worms. And to care for the earth. And the essential realisation is the need for a balance between the hand and the head.

This morning when I got up at seven the light outside was all yellow and all the elements of the world had the precise flat outlines of a Japanese print. A patch of sunlight had slipped through the curtain and lay on a postcard propped on the bookshelf. The postcard, sent to me by a friend from Istanbul, shows an Iznik tile at the Topkapi Palace, its blues and greens alive with casual arabesques. The rest of the room was still in semi-dawn darkness. I pulled back the curtain to see if more sun would flood in and saw the white window sills and frame quietly illuminated, edged by the curtain. And it made me stop and think that one thing art sometimes does is to remind us to look at just a surface for a moment and be with and see, *really see*, what is in front of us. Here and everywhere but really *really* here. Present and presence.

Art is not about the letter a woman is reading by a window but the light opening inside you; it is not about a piece of dirt or metal or clay but the remembered sensation of a rough or smooth texture under your fingertips; it is not about royalty but the human hand and its gestures; it is not the way a cabbage sits on a table or a dog walks across a street, a leaf hangs or a bug flies but a sense of movement, weight, energy, rhythm, volume, space. It is not the invisible depths of the relationship of one person to another, though it is that too, but the way light and colour affect us inside our bodies. Light doesn't need to be painted representationally to be there but it needs weight, to remind us of being alive, to be embodied, to return us to our senses. And it turns a moment into eternity, a corner of a room into something held still, like a vase, an open book or a piece of paper, a still centre of the turning world. It is almost as if we can touch time and hold it like a glass paperweight.

Our house is dotted with prints, paintings, objects and photographs, actual artworks and propped postcards of images like windows to a wider world of ideas and places. I am hungry to be transported but not move, to go but also to stay. When I travel I look for home, when I am home I often remember other places and the languages of art go on talking to me.

When travelling alone and on a small budget the first thing to do is to find the nearest market and supermarket and buy cheese, bread, yoghourt, beer – and bananas, usually from South America, calling up memories of the United Fruit Company in Gabriel Garcia Marquez's *One Hundred Years of Solitude*. Trying the new and finding echoes of the old, locating the satisfaction of handling food and drink.

Being alone means often drinking and eating alone and this is not unpleasant. I like to think of the Japanese and Chinese poets travelling, writing, drinking and celebrating their solitary lives in their work. It could be said they are doing it for everyone so those who are ground down by labour and toil know that someone somewhere is lying in the sun not worrying about where their next meal is coming from. And the next meal is found, stolen, a gift, a windfall.

Struggling to get ahead, entering the rat race and staying there, not everyone can or wants to do these things. This year I reread David Malouf's novel *The Great World*, about the life of an Australian man who spent time in Changi in a prisoner of war camp named with a sign, 'The Great World'. It was a converted fun park. He is known for his prodigious memory and returns to Australia to live beside a river at a ferry crossing bearing his father's name. The novel includes the story of his mother and how she met and married his father. The bit that has stayed with me is the description of how his mother took on her married home in all its isolation, worked hard and saw its ideal completion to a certain standard as her lifelong project, down to the last dessertspoon and curtain ring. The significant element of the story is after many years when the house is completely finished; she takes a chair and sits outside for a few days and nights, then dies. Or that is what happens in my memory of it. Some kind of metaphor for futility, it is the careful building up as well as the letting go that catches at the heart. Maybe because there is a familiarity to the desire she shows to control and order her life. In *A History of Danish Dreams*, Peter Høeg describes a woman who began to clean and could not stop, proceeding out the door of the house to sweep the very ground of the earth itself. This story too has a resonance.

On my first visit to the Venice Biennale I didn't really know what I was looking for until I found an indigenous presence in the Venezuelan pavilion. Here, in digitally manipulated photographic portraits by Antonio Briceño, were indigenous people from Venezuela, Mexico, Brazil, Peru, Colombia and Panama. The series, *Gods of America*, shows individuals embedded in the land and connected to certain places in extraordinary ways. Signed postcards were being given away too and I have one up on the wall still. It shows a man looking straight at the camera. He has a silver necklace, a headdress of vibrant green and red feathers, beads on his arms and shoulders which are black with tattoo. Behind him is a vast green land and tremendous storm clouds. On the back it says *Bepkororoti dueno de las tormantas Etnia Kayaop Brazil region floristica amazonica/Culture bringer owner of storms*. The story here is that a tapir was killed and not shared and Bepkororoti made a storm in response. It is about the importance of sharing and the interconnectedness of everything as well as the magnificence of bird feathers and the unspeakable mystery of existence.

The story often told about Australia is that it is a young country, which it isn't. New Zealand is a young country, full of steep mountains, volcanoes and waterfalls. Australia is worn down by time and weather. Some parts more than others. Asserting Australia's age as a country rather than its youth is always to draw attention to its First Peoples and the age of their cultures here. And to ask what they have learned from this longevity of occupation – what do they know, what can we learn from them, what will they teach us? There is no simple answer though every day more and more attention is paid to the significance of their long presence and their caretaking of Australia as a very very large garden. To relate to Australia's long past means learning more and more carefully about Aboriginal people's knowledge of it, listening but not appropriating, adding to our memories, word by word.

I read on a sign in a park that 'koala' is an ancient Aboriginal word meaning 'no drink'. Further research revealed that it is derived from the Dharug language as are the words dingo, wallaby, wombat, and boomerang.

I have noticed that koalas are not like you or me. When climbing trees they do not look and think that branch is too slender to support me, they just go where they want to go. And you often see them really high up wedged amongst the thinnest bendiest branches, being swayed by the wind. You rarely see them tumbling down through the tree but it must happen. And as for the magpies, the nest of sticks they built in the manna gum just over the back fence is suspended, full of air, leaning between branches, in the sky as much as on a tree.

Untitled (Bumerang mit Spiegel/Boomerang with Mirror) is an artwork made by Joseph Beuys in 1982. It contains three elements: a boomerang, a broken piece of mirror shaped roughly like a heraldic shield and a piece of string tying the two together – the mirror hangs down from one end of the boomerang making it look like a fishing rod. To me the work implies that when you look at another culture it is yourself that you see, and that one culture fishes in another.

The strangeness and exoticism of the boomerang, a simple-looking wooden tool with a magical facility almost like memory (it returns, well, actually only some boomerangs are made to return) is frequently used as a symbol for Australia, even though boomerangs have been made in ancient Egypt, Indonesia, Vanuatu, Denmark, Holland, Germany and by the Hopi Indians, the Inuit, and various peoples of India.

One of my rare uncles was a champion boomerang thrower. Years ago now he sent a boomerang in the mail that we took out onto the oval behind our house, threw straight into a tree and never saw again. I still look at that tree sometimes hoping to see that boomerang.

The North is the place where my intermingled ancestors came from, my German–Jewish father in 1940 as a refugee, my mother's Irish grandfather as a deserter from the Indian army, or so the story goes, sometime around 1910. The nation-related elements of which I am composed – British, Scottish, Irish, Jewish, Czech, Prussian, German, all northern hemisphere ones, full of stories of literature and suffering, shadowy and variegated – swim around me like silvery fish in the shallows. In my head is an art project waiting to be done about the fertility of the stereotypes that revolve around nationality. And their slipperiness.

The North is also the place of origin of the language I use most of the time. A world language, a wonderful language, and what is better than learning other languages, their words and concepts, and placing them beside the ones you know and thus expanding the world? And then there are so many Englishes. While travelling in the North, the people you meet tend think that you are English. They do not think for one minute of how much you are not English and in how many levels and layers and ways you are not and never will be. It is like being stereotyped as black or white, old or young.

The most curious comment I heard was in Germany at the Berlin Art Book Fair where I was told, by a linguistics student, that the English I spoke as an Australian (and that New Zealanders spoke too) was like a 19th century version of English because we were an island and spoke as the colonisers who first arrived had spoken. This somewhat ethnographic view (and it is refreshing for everyone to see themselves as someone else's ethnograph) seemed to ignore time, TV, movies and radio – let alone the internet and our frequent connections and travels to other places and our incorporation of other voices. And it makes us seem exotic as it casts us as segregated from the Great World.

For an exhibition called *walking on water* I made a series of plaster books cast from blue books, thus each book possessed a mottled blue skin of different tone and texture. On each book the word 'island' was repeatedly written in different languages. I typed the words on a computer, printed them on paper then cut them out, placed them face down and rubbed the back of the paper on which they were printed on the damp plaster. So they are legible, back-to-front but ghostly.

> *isola isola isola*
> *insel insel insel*
> *isla isla isla*
> *île île île*
> *eiland eiland eiland*
> *ynys, ynys, ynys*
> *island island, island*
> *eylan, eylan, eylan*
> *ostrov, ostrov, ostrov*

Fresco painting *(buon fresco)* is done on damp plaster *(intonaco)* and as the plaster 'goes off', turning from a liquid into a solid, the paint becomes part of the wall rather than merely a skin on top of it. In a small way this is what happened with the ink saying 'island' in nine different languages. The repetition was like a chant, an incantation. When you are walking on water you do look out for islands.

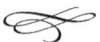

On a summer day in the seventies in Adelaide as an undergraduate student hiding from the heat I found a book by

Marie Bashkirtseff in the bowels of the Barr Smith Library at the University of Adelaide.

It seemed a secret thing to find. This is one great purpose for libraries, finds and hidden corners and alleys of books that are dusty in a special way. It seemed private and I read bits of it informally, in fragments, furtively, without checking it out, without even sitting down but propped up against the smooth grey metal of the bookshelf. Even in the seventies a woman who wanted to be an artist was virtually like being a woman who wanted to be a man. An odd very odd thought. And me wanting to be an artist was secret and what did it mean anyway. I was studying English literature, history, philosophy, politics and classical studies. I wasn't good at drawing. I hated being the centre of attention. I was never going to ingratiate myself with anyone.

And indeed maybe Bashkirtseff didn't want to be a man but wanted his freedom and status. And to live without fear. Anyway there it was, her diary full of dreams and desires, schemes and plans. It is probably still there. Bashkirtseff was a Ukrainian/Russian artist and writer living in Paris who died at the age of 25 in 1884. She had some success as an artist, showed work in the Paris Salon and has a painting in a big museum in Paris. From the perspective of today her work looks very accomplished and very conventional.

Somehow Bashkirtseff knew that her diary, kept from the age of 13 till her death, was most likely what she would be remembered by. It contains many blow-by-blow conversations and detailed daily moods and observations. At the time of first publication it was acclaimed even though it was censored by her family and even today the English translation is the bowdlerised one. Her most famous saying is 'Let us love dogs, let us love only dogs! Men and cats are unworthy creatures.'

Thirty years later at the Barr Smith Library in an exhibition called *Lost Books* I showed a series of cast plaster books. They were displayed inside glass vitrines and each book was flanked by a card with its title on it. The statement accompanying the books said that the 'fossilised' books had been found on the actual site in the heart of the University when it was excavated in 1892 to build the library. Thus suggesting that a library had been there many centuries before. Many people took it at face value.

The titles of the books were: *Early mosaics from Kangaroo Island; The North Adelaide Amphitheatre; Greek Temples on the Fleurieu Peninsula; Amphora from Port Pirie; Roman glass in Prospect; Etruscan tombs in the Adelaide Hills; Frescoes of Port Lincoln.*

They suggested that a classical Mediterranean past had been present in this place and in the countryside around it. The sensation of that distant past, its great temples with cool marble floors, classical pillars, chalky frescoes of plants, animals and dancing people, strongly incised Roman letters, forums, amphitheatres, aqueducts, statues of gods and goddesses, images of people in idealised and idiosyncratic forms was evoked by the work, as if a Pergamon Altar might be found under this southern sun.

There was in the substance of *Lost Books* too some echo of Pompeii in the way that the cavities left by bodies were filled with plaster and then displayed in museums. The story was a hoax yet included a serious consideration of how we might re-imagine other places here and how we might join them together in new ways with where we are and the stories we create.

And also in its evocation of civilisation, of thoughtful and cultured responses to specific places, a recognition of the thousands of years of Aboriginal cultures, dancing, telling stories, feasting by this river in this place.

It is two years tomorrow since the old dog died. Only recently did I realise that it was not just him I missed but the things we used to do together, the adventures based around our two daily walks, sometimes over new ground. Our walks together gathered an almost musical character. Like music their shapes had a form that could be felt in the body but was hard to put into words. They were coloured by what we saw or felt, what happened, the mood of the place. I would feel out the day and decide where to go, although Sundays was often Black Hill day. We always brought home stories and fruit, nuts, stones and shells.

It took maybe a year to remember that I like to walk, with or without a dog – though I know that walking alone is different. Without the dog walking can be more like flying, arriving somewhere with little idea how I got there. Once warmed up my legs and feet move like air. Walking with him, especially in his last years with his bad leg, each step was in doubt. We often had to sit and wait and forget about being anywhere, except sitting in the gutter breathing. And it was always more about scent than anything else, which meant lots of stopping and starting. The new dog likes circling scents, looking for food in schoolyards and meeting other dogs and people. But there's never much of a talk, just a quick hello.

JUNE

getting lost

Make the secrets productive.
Joseph Beuys

Sometimes the whole business of being an artist is what art is about. Art talks to you in many voices, sometimes literally in a human voice. It is possible that there are as many kinds of art as there are people.

In Venice I finally arrived, over the cobblestones, at the Punta della Dogana, the former customs house that is now a grand privately owned contemporary art museum. The first thing I saw in the window at the entrance was a video work by Bruce Nauman of an angry clown jumping up and down shouting '*no no no museum!*' It was totally appropriate and funny and put me in a good mood instantly.

By then I did not care much about museums or getting anywhere as weariness had overwhelmed curiosity. (This recurs in Venice and is part of the experience of being there, you get lost, you keep going, you get through it and come out on the other side in surprise or submission or something.) The clown expressing my exact mood at that moment was like a smile or a shared joke, a moment of recognition passing between two people without obligation, just humour and commiseration.

JUNE – getting lost

And the surprise of this work facing the street like a billboard instead of being inside the gallery meant that it entered my life immediately like a conversation.

And it echoed my experience of a soundwork made in 1975 by Joseph Beuys called *ja, ja, ja, ja, ja, nee, nee, nee, nee, nee (yes, yes, yes, yes, yes, no, no, no, no, no)* which I first heard in 2007 in Melbourne. I remembered finding the repetition of those simple everyday words with an aggravating German-accented whininess to be surprising, entertaining, enlivening. And somehow very personal. It's the sort of phrase you might say out loud to yourself as you walk around the house getting ready to go out. It was part of an exhibition at the National Gallery of Victoria called *Imagination Inspiration Intuition*, which brought together drawings by Beuys and by Rudolf Steiner, the founder of anthroposophy.

The centrepiece was a hundred blackboards drawn upon by Beuys, a work he first made in 1974 at the Institute of Contemporary Arts in London. It's called *Richtkräfte (Einer neuen Gesellschaft) (Directive forces (Of a new society))*. In a performance-teaching situation Beuys lectured, wrote and drew in front of an audience of students and others. As he finished each board he threw it into the middle of the gallery with a loud crash.

Writing about Beuys tends to be rapturous hagiography, foggy mysticism or sniping debunking. Surely there are other ways, lots of them. Some people are annoyed with Beuys trying to be a shaman and seeing art as able to heal society. Yet isn't art often about transformation, from raw materials to thought, from ideas into substance, from one heart or mind to another?

Both Steiner and Beuys used their drawings while talking to an audience. In Melbourne Beuys' blackboards were roughly piled into the middle of a gallery, as they had been in London, while forty-two of Steiner's drawings (made between 1919 and 1924) in coloured chalk on black paper were hung on the surrounding walls. In his life Steiner gave hundreds of lectures, erasing his blackboard drawings as he talked, but an artist called Emma Stolle got the idea of covering the blackboards with black paper thus enabling them to be kept in an archive.

Neither Steiner's nor Beuys' drawings are especially intelligible as drawings. All of them could be called *'Denkbilder'* *(thought-pictures)* as opposed to being either sensual, empirical or expressive. They are traces, residues of lectures, thus quasi-diagrams, semi-maps, rhetorical and gestural palimpsests of erasing and re-inscribing. They point rather than direct, they gather words and concepts and throw them around in symbolic and grandiose ways implying they will congeal ... and maybe when accompanying a talk they did. In some way they return us to the atmosphere of a classroom. And perhaps when you look at them you are seeing a representation of what thought looks like. A light-bulb moment here, a rushing of lines over there, a few words as picture-hangers, a circle drawing the far-flung together, everything falling apart, a persistent shape that is half-image, half-symbol, a blurry insight like the sun rising through mist.

And you might remember that Germany is said to be the land of *Dichter und Denker* (Poets and Thinkers). While in the English language only place names, a few abstract nouns and names are capitalised, in German all nouns are capitalised. This linguistic fact may well be an influence on the heaviness and depth of German or, in the case of Steiner, Austrian thought. Is this my Desk, my Book, my Face, my Thought?

Beuys often wrote words in lists amid clouds of white chalk on old worn blackboards to communicate the basic principles of his theory of social sculpture, which reflects the influence of Steiner in its insistence that creativity can be applied to all

JUNE – getting lost

aspects of human endeavour and that art can transform society. Both of them believed in the active power of 'imagination, inspiration and intuition' to lead to personal and social illumination, and beneficial change in the world – for human society, the earth and all her non-human aspects and residents.

Perhaps Beuys' most famous phrase, borrowed from 18th century German poet Novalis, is 'Everyone is an artist', which I understand as meaning everyone has the potential to be creative and to contribute their vision to society. He put it another way: 'Every sphere of human activity even peeling a potato can be a work of art as long as it is a conscious act ... everything you do contributes to the work of art that is society.'

Steiner's coloured chalk drawings are fairly pictographic. Understanding what he was getting at is not easy. Anthroposophy is not called hermetic for no reason. An example: 'Just think how dead the cosmos is when we look out there and see only burning bodies of gas that shine! Just think how alive it all becomes when we know: Those stars are expressions of love, with which the astral cosmos works on the etheric cosmos!' If this statement is translated to the instruction: 'Think of the stars not as gas but as expressions of love' it then becomes possible to understand at least a little of what he is saying and even to start to comprehend the kind of transformed encounter with the everyday he is suggesting. To take the next step might be to understand that feeling or reading animation into so-called inanimate parts of the world has a point. Many people know that there are meanings and sensations attached to the world both inside and outside us that are not accounted for by a solely scientific outlook. Isn't that some of what we can usefully learn from listening to the worldview of indigenous peoples?

In a letter reproduced in the *Imagination Inspiration Intuition* catalogue Beuys describes his task as coming from Steiner though also says he is attempting to avoid 'an overload of the Anthroposophical Museum', which he claims has often been the source of 'unconvincing even bad experiences'. His plan is to 'gradually and in his own way remove mankind's separation from and mistrust of the supernatural'. This he seeks to achieve through 'tenderness, indirectness, inconspicuousness and anti-techniques'. It is a subtle manifesto.

In Melbourne the recorded voices, of Beuys, and his long-time supporters Hennig Christiansen and Johannes Stüttgen, saying repeatedly with shifting emphasis *ja, ja, ja, ja, ja, nee, nee, nee, nee, nee* came from a nondescript felt-covered speaker, or, as it looked to me at the time, a repurposed old heater on the wall of the gallery, anyway something functional, worn and ordinary-looking. They seemed to be commenting upon and responding to the nearby blackboards in alternating agreement and disagreement, in a simple pedantic and somehow humorous expression of the ambivalence of living. And at the same time, like a one-sided conversation with someone on a telephone – maybe Sybil in *Fawlty Towers* – I know, I know, I know. *Yes, yes, yes, yes, no, no, no, no.*

The very first time I encountered Beuys's work was in 1982 when the National Gallery of Australia (NGA), then called the Australian National Gallery (ANG), first opened. An installation by Beuys was laid out along the far wall in the mysterious shadowy Sculpture Gallery, with its floor of great slabs of dark slate and shifting atmosphere of reflected watery light cast up from low windows overlooking the long pool of water outside.

I hadn't heard of Beuys and knew nothing about him. The work, *Silberstreife am Horizon* (*Stripes from the house of the Shaman*) *1964–72*, was installed behind a wall and could not be entered but only viewed from one end. Two old coats hung on the wall – Beuys' mother's sealskin fur coat turned inside out, and the coat he was wearing in 1972 when dismissed from his job at the Academy of Art in Düsseldorf. At the far end was a crude wooden structure over which were draped seven strips of thick grey felt that extended a long way on the floor toward the entry point. Five of the strips had piles of powdered pigment on the floor at their ends – one was bright-red cinnabar, one pale-yellow sulphur, and the other three were black iron phosphate. To the side lay a 'battery', a long tube of copper inside a tube of felt. The title *Silberstreife am Horizon* refers to a German proverb ('silver stripes on the horizon', meaning 'there is hope for the future', a bit like 'every cloud has a silver lining'). It also evokes what we have all seen somewhere in the world, those pieces of melting silver light far off at the horizon suggesting a dissolving sort of place where we can merge into light and our surroundings.

Grey felt is a recurring material in Beuys' work. One of his strongest stories about himself relates to being shot down in World War Two and then brought back to life by the nomadic Tatar people who wrapped him in the healing substances of fat and felt, *Fett und Filz*. It's a great story though it has often been pointed out that it is only a story, or indeed almost a dream, a creation story, an imaginary origin story. But is a great story ever only a story?

Back when I first saw the *Silberstreife* and wondered about its simplicity and use of elemental substances, it seemed to me as if everything hanging in the Australian National Gallery would stay the way it was ... for ever. This is one illusion that art galleries and museums proffer, that they will not change, that they are like Egyptian tombs – places that talk of eternity. Yet the *Silberstreife* has been packed away for many years and the artist, who came to Australia without fanfare to install it himself in 1982, died in 1986.

In Beuys' performance *How to explain art to a Dead Hare* (1965), his face was covered in gold leaf and honey, and he cradled a dead hare to which he whispered for three hours in a gallery in Düsseldorf while the audience watched from outside. Surely this work harked back to Albrecht Dürer's famous 1502 painting of a quiet young hare, as well as connecting with the idea of communication across species, something that can be seen as magical, an everyday event, or both.

Beuys said:

For me the hare is a symbol of incarnation, which the hare really enacts – something a human can only do in imagination. It burrows, building itself a home in the earth. Thus it incarnates itself in the earth: that alone is important. So it seems to me. Honey on my head of course has to do with thought. While humans do not have the ability to produce honey, they do have the ability to think, to produce ideas. Therefore the stale and morbid nature of thought is once again made living. Honey is an undoubtedly living substance – human thoughts can also become alive. On the other hand intellectualising can be deadly to thought: one can talk one's mind to death in politics or in academia.

Every time I come across Beuys' work, here and there in the world, mostly by accident, it speaks to me. Why? It is rough, it is crude, it is elemental. It might be a cobblestone, a drawing, a pressed plant with all its juices staining the paper, an old book, a glass jar or a rough sign. It is never about finesse and the artist's labour as a skilled expert, painstaking craftsperson or meticulous fanatic but uses the languages of texture, stains, living things and actual substances in a casual almost accidental way. Sometimes it's a tree. One project starting in 1982, and eventually completed by his son five years later, involved

JUNE – getting lost

planting 7000 oak trees flanked by metre-high basalt columns in Kassel, Germany. Often Beuys' work is traces of actions or props from actions. It has a homemade quality. He seemed to understand words too as his titles demonstrate. *Where would I have got if I had been intelligent* is a notable one. *The silence of Marcel Duchamp is overrated* is another that I especially like.

In Berlin at the Hamburger Bahnhof I encountered a collection of Beuys' work on permanent display that included *Umschlitt (Tallow)* – six great slabs of lard, twenty tons altogether, cast in the hollow of a pedestrian underpass originally for a sculpture exhibition in Münster in 1977 and then somehow moved. Looking like strange minimal formal sculptures they hold the tension of the congealment of their casting. It is said to have taken three months for the fat to cool down after it had been poured. Seeing them I recalled my childhood love of butter, eating it thickly and the wonder of the way it, like all fat, is the same soft texture and colour all the way through. Did the fat heal the underpass, is that why it was placed there? Yellowish white and leaning, one of the big threatening slabs is now held together with metal straps. Another has a conservator's thermometer poking out of it. As a group they are threatening and very very odd. There is a sense of imminent collapse about them. And somehow they are very much out of place, their conservation possibilities saying *no no no museum*.

Another work, *Das Ende des 20 Jahrhunderts* (*The End of the 20th Century*) involves twenty-one great rough column-shaped slabs of basalt lying around on wooden pallets or blocks of wood on the terrazzo and tiled floor. They lie the way a partially broken piece of statuary sits in a ruin, propped up to distinguish it from a piece of waste. The slabs are not set out in any design or pattern but as if they were on their way to another place and were temporarily and accidentally left in the gallery. One slab is on a trolley. Though they are unformed it feels as if they mark graves or represent human corpses. Each piece of basalt has a hand-sized circle cut into it, the hole is lined with felt and mud and the circular piece that was cut out has been polished and placed back in. The cut circles evoke rock engravings and the origins of art. The work expresses the hopelessness of making a monumental sculpture for the end of the 20th century with all its sense of unfinished business and interrupted concentration.

Over the years Beuys made many multiples in large and small editions, they were often very simple things or existing objects that he slightly altered, for example a small open wooden box with the word *Intuition* written inside it in pencil. You could easily make one yourself from an old drawer. Somewhere there is a photo of Beuys signing *Intuition* boxes outside the Düsseldorf Academy of Art while sitting next to a great stack of them. There are said to be about 12,000 of them in the world. They are props for thinking. When you see one you might think, well it is just an empty wooden box but also that intuition is real but not visible.

Another artwork presented in the first hang at the National Gallery of Australia was Bruce Nauman's *The true artist helps the world by revealing mystic truths*. It is a spiral of pink neon within which the words of its title run cursively in blue neon. The smarty-pants aspect of its full title, which includes the words (*Window or wall sign*), emphasises the commodity nature of the artwork – you can place it in a window or on a wall, whichever form suits you, it is flexible enough to fit your space, like any other consumer item.

Yet this flexibility contradicts the notion of a mystical truth that we surely do not choose, and that we expect to not really suit us but to slide up on us either suddenly, like a shaft of blue light, or slowly through long preparation. Even so, it would still be unpredictable or sharp when it arrived. And such things cannot, by definition, be easily conveyed to others. Nauman is ambivalent – he believes what the sign says but also finds it unbelievable. Isn't a mystic truth something that is embedded in an experience, not something that can be glibly stated, easily understood, bought or found in a gallery? And yet.

The dog does not bury his bones but keeps them on the front veranda, tiled with dull-red terracotta quarry tiles. Of course I kick them into the nearby clump of wild fennel but he slowly retrieves them for thoughtful nightly sessions on the doormat.

On the veranda is some furniture found on the street – an old red cane chair, a round cane table, a wooden art nouveau plant stand painted thickly with faded white paint, and an olive-green bookshelf holding garden tools and pieces of weathered enamelware as well as brass and copper potholders in various stages of verdigris. There are four family heirloom blue-and-white Delft tiles propped up on the ancient air conditioner that pokes out of the window, an old bicycle, and two wooden chairs. There are two coir doormats, one for the dog and one for your feet. A few glaucous succulent plants in pots decorate the edges of the verandah and the pillars. Rounded white pieces of delicately patterned coral and a vivid fossil of a fern sit near a few seashells and a small terracotta dog with a thick grey-green textured glaze. A shiny white glazed terracotta duck shaped like a Mesopotamian duck weight is curled in the corner, and just off the verandah a blue-and-green-glazed terracotta cat sits very still.

This part of the house is where tea is taken, books are read, and breakfast, lunch or dinner can be eaten in great privacy.

Because of the brush fence covered in ivy and the dense trees in the front garden the veranda is invisible from the street. Flanking the verandah is a cumquat tree planted by my mother. It is always flowering or fruiting, scenting the air with its white blossom or bright orange globes. The old ashleaf maple tree that stretches long arms in every direction has some dead branches but could not be said to be anything but happy. The Robyn Gordon grevillea has grown so much that it has gone from looking like a single bush to a row of bushes. It flowers for months on end attracting birds from the beginning of winter to the end of spring. And then there is the native hibiscus from Eyre Peninsula with its purple trumpet flowers. It too has been allowed to become straggly and untidy.

Only native plants flagged as drought resistant find a place in this garden. They come from the Belair National Park Native Plants Nursery where rows and rows of seedlings are ranged down the side of the hill. The location of the origin of each seed is written by hand near the plants. The printed arrow-shaped white plastic labels telling a story in a few words about the plant's habits and history are a form of found poetry. And while they have botanical names sometimes they also have colloquial names and some, like wandoo, talyuberlup, moort, illyarrie, belah, yorrell, coolibah, punty and mulga, have names from different Aboriginal languages.

I love going to this park. It is large and has all kinds of bush as well as tennis courts, barbeques, ovals, walks, a playground and the governor's summer house. Once we walked there and lost the dog which reappeared chasing an emu. Another time when I was sitting at a picnic table, a kookaburra flew straight at my face. A few times we saw a big old man kangaroo right near the car park. But it is being in the nursery, reading these laconic poems, walking the aisles of seedlings and saplings, and dreaming of planting trees, which refreshes and soothes me. I would like to buy and plant them all. It is a great moment when you shake a tree you have planted and it is so firm in the earth that it doesn't move.

The dog and I sometimes stand on the edge of the front veranda at night and look at the stars. It is always good to sense him down there close to me. Occasionally when I am not well and the night is long we go out together and stand under the stars and then come back inside, lie down and think about them being up there past the roof looking down at us.

JULY
inside books

If we opened people up, we'd find landscapes.
Agnes Varda

Travelling, I sometimes say, is like dying, you have to say goodbye and you can't take much with you. It pares you back to yourself and what you are prepared to carry. It throws you into the moment, and out of habit. I know they say you can't take anything with you when you die, but actually you take everything you have never said, and all your memories.

The importance of books when travelling cannot be emphasised enough. An electronic device is not the same, it treats books as words alone and disregards their physical attributes such as scent and heft and texture. You can crush or hug them, dogear their pages, pile them up or throw them across the room or in a bin. Seeing someone reading a book at a bus stop or in a park under a tree is like seeing someone in a secret place.

Locating a second-hand English bookshop in a foreign city is a bit like going home. I have been lucky enough to do it in Florence, Prague, Berlin, Oxford, Beijing and London. When in Santiago, Chile, in a new bookshop, I was ridiculously surprised to find all the books were in Spanish – but treasured still what the words *Historia de La Vida Privada* could make me think. Even walking through a library can help the homesick, their sense of freedom of information and the ambience of a forest of ideas and stories is consoling.

When travelling, taking notes and writing is a way of holding the moment and saving the sights. It is also like drawing in some way, a physical pouring of ink or pencil onto paper, producing lines and scrawls that are voices. But there is never an exact account, there are always damned huge spaces between the words and my memories when I look later hoping to find clear all-encompassing pictures.

And what do we take with us? *what we bring with us*, an exhibition I had in Melbourne in 2006, included paintings of vessels made in acrylic paint from memory on vinyl long-playing records. To me the vases and jugs, teapots and coffeepots, bowls and cups evoked my mid-20th-century-modern childhood and adolescence, its meals and flowers, silent moments and shadows on walls.

Just as looking at the vessels can make me a child again so somehow the overcrowded shelves of my home library and my memories of books travel with me along with their words. Propped up somewhere nearby is always the worn book, *Collected Poems 1909–1933* by T.S. Eliot, hard cloth cover, no dustjacket, its thin bookbinder's cloth an inky kind of royal blue. It was published by Faber & Faber in 1936, and given to my father during the Second World War, by a friend. It is inscribed: 'As An Answer to your last letter, 12th May, 1942. Franz.'

Franz Lebrecht was a social democrat German Jewish intellectual whom my father met in an internment camp in Tatura, near Shepparton in Victoria. Refugees, stateless people and aliens, like my father, who came to Australia from the UK on HMT *Dunera* in 1940 were sent to such camps all over Australia. The case of the *Dunera* is a significant part of

Australian history in the Second World War. Two thousand refugees, mostly Jewish men who had fled the Nazis, were packed into this British passenger ship which had capacity for 1600. They were badly mistreated by their British guards who were later court-martialled and it is considered a notorious case of wartime injustice.

Lebrecht was arrested in Berlin in 1934 while placing flowers on the grave of Rosa Luxemburg on her birthday. He then spent four years in concentration camps and was released after an impressive conversation with Adolf Eichmann, or so the story goes. He somehow left Germany and ended up in internment camp in Australia after spending some time in Malaya. Later in life he lived in Berlin with his wife Hildegard. Somewhere there must be letters. I can easily picture his smiling intelligent face.

Marxist theorist, philosopher, economist and revolutionary socialist, Rosa Luxemburg's best-known saying is: *Freedom is always the freedom of the one who thinks differently* (*Freiheit ist immer Freiheit der Andersdenkenden*), or in other words, *freedom is always the freedom of the dissenter*. Or in other words, *freedom is about non-conformity*. She was assassinated on 15 January 1919 after a failed socialist uprising in Berlin.

I was thinking that it was Luxemburg who wrote: 'If I can't dance I don't want to be in your revolution', but that was Emma Goldman. Born in Russia but working mostly in North America, Goldman was an anarchist, renowned public speaker and lecturer, activist, nurse, writer, thinker. Told off once for dancing and having too much fun she wrote:

> *I want freedom, the right to self-expression, everybody's right to beautiful, radiant things. Anarchism meant that to me, and I would live it in spite of the whole world – prisons, persecution, everything. Yes, even in spite of the condemnation of my own closest comrades I would live my beautiful ideal.*

JULY – inside books

Luxemburg did write in a letter from prison:

I suppose I must be out of sorts to feel everything so deeply. Sometimes, however, it seems to me that I am not really a human being at all, but like a bird or a beast in human form. I feel so much more at home even in a scrap of garden like the one here, and still more in the meadows when the grass is humming with bees than at one of our party congresses.

In 1912, Goldman started *Mother Earth*, an anarchist journal. She and her lover planned the murder of industrialist and financier Henry Clay Frick, whose grand art-filled house is now the Frick Museum, located east of Central Park in New York. Frick was once known as the most hated man in America, because of his harsh anti-union strikebreaking tactics.

The Frick Museum describes itself as one of the world's most perfect museums. Hmmm. After reading about it, in my imagination it was a light-filled place of taste and beauty, of wide passages and airy spaces, domestic in the sense of having been primarily a home and therefore having furnished rooms that were also galleries. Thus gracious to a human scale. A bit like my house but bigger.

When I got there I found it to be a cluttered place with ugly furniture and way too many artworks on show, a few of which are great. Curiously Frick wrote about the house: 'We desire a comfortable well-arranged home, simple, in good taste, and not ostentatious.' If only. I expected a series of calm and beautiful rooms with natural light tilting into them, something like the place some Vermeers make you imagine, with reflected glimmers sent up by a canal below, a radiant illumination that has bounced off water to slip through the window and hit smooth – perhaps yellow – walls and slide into a room where there is more space than stuff, and everything is serene.

The one work on show in the Frick Museum that met my expectations and truly radiated light to me was *The Ecstasy of Saint Francis*, which Giovanni Bellini painted in 1478–1479. A strange intense unearthly light fills the work. It is the cool-blue light of dawn with its yellow tinges before the sun is up; the time when indirect light is everywhere but the sun is not yet burning in the sky. Saint Francis seems to have just stood up from a desk outside a cave where he has been reading the Bible and contemplating death in the form of a skull. The hills, the olive tree on the left with its watershoots, the slender new fig tree, the plantain, the yellow-flowering evening primrose, a general weedy unkempt look, means this could be my garden (if a koala was hanging around in a distant gum tree and a black-and-white dog was lying by the step). The light is very glaucous, very blue, very unearthly. It creates a huge inbreathing stillness in this moment.

The story depicted by Bellini is thought to be Saint Francis at the moment of receiving the stigmata or meditating on the creation of the world and thus perhaps singing his 'Canticle of the Sun', also known as the 'Canticle of the Creatures'. His mouth is open, he could well be singing. A complete world surrounds him yet is still. It is as if he sees everything in the painting as well as simply being in that moment, as if his breath has held everything motionless. And you stand there like him, lost in contemplation of the miracle of the world.

As far as actual creatures go there is a distant flock of sheep with a shepherd, a donkey in the middle distance and a strange-looking hare poking its head through the rocks behind him. Though Saint Francis is famous for preaching to the birds here there is only one, a heron that pauses as herons do, and stares into the water. After this viewing I had one of the best meals that I found in New York, a bread roll with butter and a cup of tea with honey in it. I imagined Saint Francis would have appreciated the simplicity of this meal and its peaceable reception by my stomach.

How does Bellini's painting connect to the worn poetry book covered in inky-blue bookbinder's linen that I began to read so many years ago? Maybe its blueness?

I think it was a combination of the book's appearance as well as its words that first impressed me. Its paper is fine and laid – the lines of the wire of the tray on which the paper was made are just visible in their even unevenness, the paper is cream-coloured and crisp, the typesetting spacious. No one had spoken to me of modernism or what a person needed to know. I just found the book on the shelf at home and liked the look and feel of it. It felt and smelled good. And *The Waste Land* is in there among other poems like *The Love Song of J. Alfred Prufrock, Portrait of a Lady, Ash Wednesday, The Hollow Men*, and *Journey of the Magi*.

I claimed it, took it over, read it, and wrote translations in pencil of the French, Italian, Greek and Latin words in it. I don't know why I became so attached to it. It was like making a thoughtful and mysterious friend.

As a talisman, as consolation: what were the words I collected and hung onto and why? And why are they some of the words that still, forty years later, especially when I am travelling, echo in my head and return to me like fragments of wisdom from an old relative? Did my old relatives ever really get a chance to say anything much to me? Not really, I only ever met a few briefly, but something may emerge as I write. They probably tried. I'm sure my father wanted to pass on fragments of insight, such as not worrying about what other people think, about being yourself, specialising in something, getting on with living … but it is difficult to give advice. How do you give what you have learned to another? The unplanned moments, the slivers of experience holding some insight that you feel rather than recall fully, are often the most precious.

> *... when we came back, late, from the Hyacinth garden,*
> *Your arms full, and your hair wet, I could not*
> *Speak, and my eyes failed, I was neither*
> *Living nor dead, and I knew nothing,*
> *Looking into the heart of light, the silence.*

Why do I still lean on these lines from that particular old book? I recall, somehow, deciding then and there that it was what I thought and felt these words from *The Waste Land* meant that was important, not what someone else was going to tell me. This was a watershed moment, something like realising that if I was going to write something it had to be what I really meant not what I thought I was meant to write. It was like throwing off a rope that was binding my arms, like pushing a stone off my shoulders.

A few other lines from that book that come back to me again and again are:

> *I am moved by fancies that are curled*
> *Around these images and cling:*
> *The notion of some infinitely gentle*
> *Infinitely suffering thing.*

I saw this as a description of the way smoke winds around something and leaves a scent, and always that the 'suffering thing' was me. Now I recall my father telling me to stop suffering, but that was always hard around him. Though suffering can be a habit as much as a response. I guess Eliot probably was thinking of religion or art, the writing of poetry or indeed simply the earth. It's a speculative line that rests in reverie. And the poem it is in, *Preludes*, describes solitary people in a city waking up or coming home from work. It ends with the words:

> *Wipe your hand across your mouth, and laugh;*
> *The worlds revolve like ancient women*
> *Gathering fuel in vacant lots.*

And now I am older, if not yet ancient, and when I gather bark or wood in the backyard or in the park from under trees I sense I am doing something very old that is making the worlds revolve. And everyone knows it is old women who keep the world turning. Or is it all women? This was borne out in an extraordinary way at the inaugural opening of MONA, the Museum of Old and New Art in Hobart in 2011 when a half-open door, probably undiscovered by some, led to a space, the literal and metaphorical power room of the Museum. Here behind the mesh protecting the machines were women of all ages dressed in white, spinning and singing.

I get the same feeling when I pick fruit, garden or cook. Once I prepared olives for preserving by soaking them in water for forty days. I felt a calm emotional pleasure in tipping out the water and replacing it daily. There is something about ritual and repetition, about a simple responsibility or obligation, about handling things with movements that are purposeful and gentle, and have been repeated over many years by many people. These lines of poetry contain acceptance, and involve, however laterally, something about endurance and the birth and experience of compassion, infinitely gentle, infinitely suffering.

Maybe that is what Franz was trying to tell my father.

And while I am thinking of old poetry books there is my

Ezra Pound *Selected Poems* ... a beaten-up silvery grey-and-black Faber & Faber 1959 paperback, selected and introduced by T.S. Eliot in 1928, that I bought for 10 cents in 1975, and in which I marked with a pencilled X all those poems that created a shiver in me.

And over the time I am writing these words I lose and find that book and others several times and must always be getting down on the floor and looking through piles of books or along shelves and then standing up again, still looking but somehow altered by the search. This is normal. Without a hunt, a physical encounter with the object, the bookshelves with their dust, their treasures, their stories and their peculiar order (certainly not Dewey but more like a garden or a painting where your eyes get used to a certain configuration of colours and shapes so that you notice if something has moved), a book is not really found. Landscape is like this too, and even the sky. You must lie on the floor or the earth from time to time and when you do sometimes you must forget what you are looking for and just be.

My relationship with Pound has endured over the years, though I certainly haven't read all his work. Only recently I saw his photo and read more about him. It was not the person or the personality that I was drawn to, or even the poetry as a whole, but certain words, moods, energies in his early poetry.

Recently I learnt that what I thought were Pound's poems in the series called *Cathay* (an old word for China), published in 1915 in a print run of 1000, were actually poems he 'translated' from Chinese.

The poems in *Cathay* are described as being written by Rihaku, a Japanese name for the Chinese poet Li Bai also known as Li Po. On the title page it says: 'CATHAY/ Translations by Ezra Pound / For the most part from the Chinese of Rihaku, from the notes of the late Ernest Fenellosa, and the decipherings of the Professors Mori and Ariga.' All very vague and I simply overlooked it in the past on my way to the poetry. Fenellosa was the son of a Spanish pianist. He grew up in America and became an expert in Japanese art and poetry. So is it Chinese poetry or by Pound? Is it a translation; is it both? How does it mingle China and Japan? Is it Orientalism – an idea about the East rather than the actuality, or the many actualities? Is it authentic, or at least an accurate transposition of an aesthetic? And who are Mori and Ariga, who disappear as soon as they arrive?

The poets of Li Po's time were determined amateurs who painted, wrote, went for walks, got drunk, and then wrote about all of that and the simple domestic moments of their lives. In a poem called *Epitaphs* in Pound's collection *Lustra* the legendary end of Fu I's life appears:

> *Fu I loved the high cloud and the hill,*
> *Alas, he died of alcohol.*

As well as that of Li Po.

> *And Li Po also died drunk.*
> *He tried to embrace a moon*
> *In the Yellow River.*

Fenellosa's widow gave her husband's Li Po translation notes to the thirty-year-old Pound, trusting him because of his poetry. Pound was an enthusiast, a writer, an editor, who started magazines, found money for writers he thought needed to write, and was instrumental in the publishing of T.S. Eliot and James Joyce. During the Second World War he got into trouble by broadcasting in Italy in support of Mussolini, was imprisoned for this (which included three weeks in an outdoor steel cage), accused of treason and ended up in a mental asylum in America for twelve years. He spent the last fourteen years of his life living in Venice, mostly in silence it is said.

When Pound was arrested in Italy in 1945 he was allowed to take three books with him – a Chinese text of Confucius, a translation of it and a Chinese dictionary. The only other thing he took with him was a eucalyptus seedpod, a gumnut. He mentions it – 'eucalyptus for memory' in one of his *Pisan Cantos*, echoing Ophelia's words: 'rosemary for remembrance'. It enabled him to remember Italy rather than Australia but is still a link.

Pound's passion for poetry meant seeing it as an important human activity spanning and crossing all cultures and times. He had an encyclopedic nature and applied himself to reading all the poetry that he could, in whatever language it was written. His goal was: 'By the age of thirty to have read all the poetry in the world.'

'Make it new' was his motto, though what he meant by it is possibly rather more like 'make it fresh'. It is said that the phrase 'make it new/fresh' is not originally Pound's but that its source is a historical anecdote about Ch'eng T'ang, first king of the Shang dynasty (1766–1753 BC), who had his washbasin inscribed with this motto, thus mixing the practical and the metaphorical.

There is a certain mood in the *Cathay* poems that touches me deeply, a mood of melancholy, exile and submission to custom and circumstances. Which of course I think of as Chinese and ineluctably connected to that unimaginably long and complicated Chinese history and experience I will never know. And it is linked to the China that lives in my imagination, vast and unknowable, subtle and pragmatic, secretive and evasive, wonderful in food and ceramics, self-contained and full of the weight of human suffering.

JULY – inside books

There are words in this book that I carry with me always in my memory as friends, companions, company.

Like this excerpt from *The Exile's Letter* written by Li Po, and Pound.

> *And if you ask how I regret that parting:*
> *It is like the flowers falling at Spring's end*
> *Confused, whirled in a tangle.*
> *What is the use of talking, and there is no end of talking,*
> *There is no end of things in the heart.*

And today the rain on the roof was like footsteps.

Most people have a certain breed of dog running in their family and stick to it with loyalty. When I thought about getting another dog I figured that the right dog would appear. And so it happened, he was out there and I did find him. In fact I went to look at another dog, it was being adopted when I arrived so they looked at me, said wait here and went to get a short brindle Staffy that barked a lot. Take him for a walk they said. While we were walking by the side of the country road three volunteer dog walkers on their way home stopped their cars to tell me what a dear he was. When we got back someone else was thinking of taking him so although I had been going just to look that day, I ended up with a new friend. Three years ago now.

In the beginning he would not meet my gaze but now he will look deeply at me with his amber eyes. Much of the time he sleeps in a big armchair next to my desk. The animal shelter told me that his name was Onyx, he has a lovely brown-and-black brindle coat but I have called him Eno, after the musician

Brian Eno. When he first came we listened to a lot of Eno's music, especially the ambient work *Thursday Afternoon*, which has the quality of slowing your breathing and thoughts. I can think and write to it and he can snooze. It was originally made to accompany Eno's video paintings. On YouTube someone called Jonathan Jolly has put it up with time-lapse footage of clouds coloured in purple, pink and turquoise. Eno sees his music as addressing the parasympathetic part of the nervous system, which deals with 'digest and rest, calm down and connect things together'. I have lost track of the number of people that I have met while walking Eno, and told about his music.

AUGUST
finding wildness

So long as you write about what you wish to write, that is all that matters; and whether it matters for ages or only for hours, nobody can say.
Virginia Woolf

After flying from Adelaide I walked to the National Gallery of Art in Ottawa and right in front of it discovered a Taiga Garden (*Le Jardin Boréal*) full of whistling buzzing sound. Taiga (a Russian kind of word with Turkish links) describes a far northern hemisphere evergreen forest of conifers, such as pines, spruces and larches.

A sense of warm energetic life embodied in the voices of crickets, cicadas and frogs whirring together drew me into this garden expecting and hoping to find frogs. I located the source of the noise, a speaker in a tree, but still found much delight in the evocative aural intensity of being in the Taiga. I sat at its edge to eat my snack of bread and bananas, and then saw two of the blackest squirrels in the world vibrating their question-mark tails and chasing each other up and down through the trees.

The garden was designed in 1988 by landscape architect Cornelia Hahn Oberlander, who arrived in Canada at eighteen as a refugee from Nazi Germany and became a pioneer in green design and rooftop landscapes. The Taiga Garden has a wonderful scrubby quality. This patch of land edged by a ridge of very big flat grey rocks and planted not only with trees but many grasses, groundcovers and shrubs (a sign lists arctic bluegrass, cotton grass, wild strawberry, red-leafed rose, bog rosemary, Canadian dwarf cinquefoil, Tartarian dogwood, Austrian pine, dwarf Mugho pine, Siberian cypress, blue flag iris and Vancouver jade kinnikinnick) has a strong atmosphere and presence. It stands in for all the wild land to the north of Ottawa, and in other countries of the northern hemisphere too, places of great space and big skies, though not necessarily silence. It has the free feeling of a certain kind of wildness — or is it wilderness?

Oberlander, who has written about the solace of trees, said she was inspired by a 1913 painting by A.Y. Jackson called *Terre Sauvage (Wild Land)*. Jackson was a member of the Group of Seven, also known as the Algonquin Group, seven male painters said to have 'discovered' the Canadian landscape in the early 20th century. Emily Carr, the one woman who was almost, but not quite, in the Group, is now the best known of all, certainly outside Canada, chiefly for her paintings of totem poles from Canadian indigenous cultures. Unlike the Group of Seven she lived in the west of Canada and went to many of the remote places on the Pacific Northwest where the poles were located.

Carr became a writer as well as an artist when she was recovering from illness and told to rest. The title of her first book, a memoir *Klee Wyck*, means 'the laughing one' in Ucluelet, a local indigenous language.

In the National Gallery in Ottawa I found, as I did in other national galleries around the world, some kind of principle of resemblance. It means many artworks by artists you have not heard of are full of the echoes of Australian artists that you do know, in this case I noted John Glover, Arthur Streeton, David Davies, John Peter Russell. You can walk along and tick them off in your head as you go. Among all the paintings, Carr's work stands out powerfully. It has a great graphic force that may be compared to that of Australia's Margaret Preston, who also spent a lot of time looking at indigenous culture and responding to it.

The book by Carr that I have read is her posthumously published *Growing Pains*, an amusing and personal account of her experiences as a Canadian, a woman and an artist. These three parts of her identity mark her survival through family, genteel society and poverty. She worked on her art in Canada, in England where she was called 'Motor' by fellow art students, in France and until her death in Canada. In photographs Carr is a tremendously fierce-looking woman, large, assertive and defensive. Her chief companions were often animals, she camped out with them in a caravan on painting expeditions, she even had a monkey. At the very end of the book she paints a moving self-portrait of herself when she describes an old wild duck no longer able to fly with the flock and so left behind, not sad or asking for pity, but staying on the ground making the strong honking noises of joy that the ducks make when they fly south for the winter.

Carr painted what she saw as sites of both cultural loss and cultural endurance, her first inspiration was the forest and then the incredible carved wooden totem poles made by different groups of Pacific Northwest indigenous people. She made difficult solo journeys to locate and record them. When she applied to the government to fund further work she was refused, her work deemed not scientific enough.

She painted lots of other things before returning to painting the poles again later in life. Finally, when she wanted to work but could not afford too many expensive materials, she worked on paper with thin oil paint and developed her own expressive vision of the forest. These works have a close equivalence to some of the art of Vincent Van Gogh in that they make visible a shifting swirling emotional energy in the land and the sky. There is a bit of Georgia O'Keefe here too but Carr's work is much more expressive. Carr was an outsider, though not an outsider artist, frank about her separateness and the focus that enabled her to keep working.

I was in Ottawa, the Canberra of Canada, to see *Sakahàn*, the first quinquennial exhibition of international indigenous art. Among many diverse works the recurring presence of drawing was noticeable. Lots and lots of often awkward drawing, some of which was good in spite of – or because of – its 'badness', drawing as recording, thinking and communication, drawing serving its function as a voice of authenticity.

Though not part of *Sakahàn*, the artwork of William Noah, in the Inuit Art Gallery located inside the National Gallery, was among the best I saw. His drawings of places, tasks and objects had purpose and need in them. His work clearly influenced two Inuit artists who were in *Sakahàn*, Annie Pootoogook and Itee Pootoogook, as their work followed a similar documentary turn. Best of all, in *Sakahàn*, were the six coloured pencil and watercolour works *Seasonal Changes in the Amazon Forest* by Colombian indigenous Nonuya artist Abel Rodriguez (Mogaje Guiju). They depict vivid intimate memories of an environment of plants, trees and animals. His deep knowledge of the forest learnt from his uncle as a namer of plants has meant that he has worked as a guide for Tropenbos, an international organisation based in the Netherlands working to improve the management and sustainability of tropical forests. He had to leave the forest because of violence against indigenous people there.

He now lives in Bogotá, where again he has been working for Tropenbos making drawings and a downloadable book that is an inventory of *The plants cultivated by the people from the center in the Colombian Amazon*. Though his work has been included in several contemporary art exhibitions he does not consider himself to be making contemporary art but said: 'We don't really have that concept, but the closest one I can think of is *iimitya*, which in Muinane means 'word of power' – all paths lead to the same knowledge, which is the beginning of all paths.'

On my way to the National Gallery I visited the Ottawa Arts Court and saw *In the Flesh*, an exhibition by four Canadian indigenous artists in which one work, *Buffalo Bone China* by Dana Claxton, showed an historic film loop of buffalo running. On the floor in front of it was a pile of broken bone china. The work memorialises the cruel and wasteful decimation of thousands of the buffalo that First Nations people hunted and relied upon for so much. Some buffalo bones were exported to England to be used in the making of fine bone china. It was a simple and powerful juxtaposition but its chief impact on me was the film, both mesmerising and heart-breaking, especially the sight of the very young buffalo doing its best to keep up.

The next day I walked through a produce market where many stallholders cheerfully greeted me with 'Bonjour, Madame'. Then I talked to Benjamin, a high school volunteer guide standing in the gardens near Parliament House helping visitors find their way. The elegant grey-roofed buildings that I had thought were Parliament House turned out to be a hotel. Benjamin gave me a short history of the Rideau Canal built by the French and the Irish. And I realised how very little I know about Canadian history.

I walked past a beggar and his two dogs, he spoke to me in French then English. I saw a sign on a post saying: 'No to panhandling – Yes to giving'. I crossed over the Royal Alexandra Interprovincial Bridge into Gatineau, Quebec, to get to the Canadian Museum of Civilisation. On the bridge I exchanged greetings with a man with a dog pushing a wagon within which was a large white cat. The dog lifted its front paws like a circus dog. At the far end of the bridge a First Nations man sat on the ground. We said hello to each other too. The cars on the bridge sounded like bees.

The Museum of Civilization is a grey building of low flat horizontal loops built in 1989 and designed by Douglas Cardinal, a Métis and Blackfoot Canadian architect. It was surrounded by great quantities of low bushy grasses within which metal stakes held up blank metal signs suggesting better days, severe weather or theft. But I respected their emptiness, their refusal to speak. Such silence creates space to think.

Yet this museum was not staying still. As part of a reflective culture its name was changed to the Canadian Museum of History just two months after I was there. It has changed its name several times since it opened. It started as the Geological Survey of Canada display hall in 1859, was the National Museum of Canada from about 1910 to 1968, then the National Museum of Man from 1968 to 1986, and the Canadian Museum of Civilization from 1986 to 2013. Its current plan is to focus on Canadian and world history. Here I sat outside the café with a cup of tea and a roll, and a sparrow and a mottled grey-brown seabird came straight up to me to share. When I said there was no more they went away.

I looked at a temporary exhibition on voodoo with a bit of trepidation, being careful of inadvertent bewitchment and noticing some strange odours, but my special interest, my chief purpose, was to see the grand space devoted to Canada's indigenous people, the First Peoples Hall. A number of very big totem poles and recreations of six different Pacific Coast houses were there, as well a very large pure-white plaster sculpture called *The Spirit of Haida Gwaii* by British Columbia Haida artist Bill Reid. This six-metre-long dugout canoe is crowded with passengers – Raven, Mouse Woman, Grizzly Bear, his human wife Bear Mother, their cubs Good Bear and Bad Bear, Beaver, Dogfish Woman, Eagle, Frog, Wolf, the Ancient Reluctant Conscript (a small male human paddler) and a human shaman. A nearby sign says: 'The variety and interdependence of the canoe's occupants represents the natural environment on which the ancient Haida relied for their survival: the passengers are diverse, and not always in harmony, yet they depend on one another to live.' The strong shapes of the canoe's varied occupants, like the totem poles, express the energy of a vibrant life force by paying homage to the diversity and beauty of the world. The accompanying explanation emphasises the complexity of living together in any culture.

What made me especially want to see the totem poles? Apart from the paintings of Emily Carr I think it was a favourite rather crushed black-and-white photocopy that I have of a photograph from a book whose name I have forgotten of a totem pole somewhere in Canada. It shows a huge carved animal looming into the sky and near it a huge human figure reaching out. The sight of them as landmarks would have been a remarkable daily event. And the suggestion of a close symbiosis between humans and their environment draws me in.

Canada is full of forests. Totem poles are carved cedar trees, the interlocked animals and faces that they often contain emphasise metamorphosis and interchangeability. Any elbow or knee, any fold or bend, will have a face, nose or ears tucked into it. As your eye moves up and down or across it, you experience strength, energy, rhythm and delight in the diverse shapes of the world. I looked intently at the carved animals and faces, trying to connect with and somehow absorb their inspiring energy — something they have in turn collected from the world and made concrete. Imagine travelling up a river in a boat and seeing the great carvings along the banks.

The greeting to the First Peoples Hall says:

Welcome We are the first peoples

We include Inuit, First Nations and Métis. Together we have often been called Native. Now we are more often known collectively as Aboriginal.

It has been hard to find an acceptable common name because we are in fact hundreds of distinct peoples. Each of these peoples has its own name, language, ancestral lands and culture.

Today we live on reserves and in hamlets, towns and cities across Canada. We are connected with one another by our survival as Aboriginal peoples through the last 500 years. We also maintain our connection with our lands, and strive to keep our languages alive and our cultures vital in the modern world.

Welcome to the First Peoples Hall.

I include these words in full because I know that people need to speak for themselves and that it is important to listen to them. And because an important part of what is clearly being said here is the often unacknowledged or unknown multiplicity of First Peoples.

The sample model houses alongside the totem poles in the museum are made of great amounts of wood. In one room huge planks are stitched together to form a wall, in another one, pillars covered in strong repeated chisel marks hold up a giant beam with similar markings. How does looking at dwellings, dishes and clothes, necklaces and shoes, replicas of houses,

AUGUST – finding wildness

photographs and other bits and pieces add up to respecting or knowing more about cultures? I don't know but I go on doing it.

A significant part of the First Peoples' story in Canada are the Métis, the descendants of First Nations women and French, English or Scottish fathers, who are now considered a distinct Aboriginal people. Louis Riel, hanged for high treason in 1885 while fighting for Métis recognition, spoke memorably: 'My people will sleep for 100 years and when they awaken it will be the artists who give them back their spirit.'

And I wonder about my people, where are they, who are they? As a person put together from several diasporas with small families it is no simple thing to belong somewhere. How do we know where we belong, how do we belong?

My domestic version of wildness is a certain slanting afternoon light through tree branches into an apparently neglected garden, a place where time is stopped. Where a white chair is filled with leaves and water has collected in buckets and old saucepans. A wild garden, a wilderness garden, a secret enchanted garden.

In gardens is slow time, vegetable time. The garden is an expression of wildness; it has stillness and hiding places. Beneath that bush of lavender or rosemary, for example, lying on the ground, wound around its grey trunk, you might stop and breathe deeply without thinking. You might stop breathing altogether. The dirt has its own scent into which you may go for a while. When wet it changes. To get to the scent you need to raise it to your nostrils or lie down flat.

Then there is the tree you may stand behind or touch in the same place every day, thus coming to know it. There are the scented plants you can crush, and the snails sleeping in their shells, dormant behind a thin shiny skin of stuff. When it rains suddenly they are everywhere in all sizes gliding in all directions so you must watch where you step. There are the crickets in summer that start up with rain or sprinklers then stop their regular chirp when you step nearby. There are the ants bent on world domination, streaming in countless numbers, storing their unborn children in the roots of plants in pots, moving them one egg at a time after the watering. There are the geckos, spotted and spangled with irregular patterns, living under and inside wooden boxes and old pots.

After I write these words I sit on the front veranda to eat a bowl of soup and the crested pigeon bringing up two young ones in the front garden comes and speaks directly to me with nods and looks about supplying them with food, like I used to when I had a regular job. Later in the day I walk to the supermarket and buy a medium-sized bag of wild birdseed.

In late August spring is well underway, and the alert can learn birdcalls of satiation, birth and satisfaction. The rosella with its bright red head gives a real chirp of gladness. There is also alarm and hostility. From observation I have discerned that being a bird is not all about freedom and flight but frequently homelessness, fear, and constant alertness. Thrown out of the nest as early as possible, life is a constant search for what is food and what is not, for mates, for home, for somewhere to spend the night. Friends and relatives are killed in front of your eyes by cats or cars. A simple bath needs careful vigilance.

I greatly enjoyed watching the tender childhoods of a family of crested pigeons. Sitting in the pea straw I spread around as mulch, the two young ones would lean on each other, their wrinkled eyes drooping and closing. Now they are gone and a pile of feathers is scattered under the wormwood bush.

Today a single pigeon and a piping shrike bathed cautiously together in the birdbath and it made me think that it might be the case that birds make alliances or form friendships with birds of other types when they have lost their families. For company, for companionship.

My suburb, Erindale, got its name from an Irish man who had a property here that he named after his home in Ireland. Erin means Ireland or green water. Dale means an open valley. When the South Australian Company came to survey and sell land around Adelaide it was the fertile place of big trees and readily available water to the east of the city, where the five creeks leading into the River Torrens run through the foothills, that was favoured. How the Company could sell land they didn't buy from the original residents is hard to understand.

In some ways it is hard to 'see' the past when walking around here; in other ways it is not hard at all. It is less than 200 years since South Australia was proclaimed a British colony in 1836. Erindale was subdivided in 1912, our house was built in 1925, and added to in 1964. In early photographs or paintings of this place I can easily recognise the hills in the background. They are park-like, consistent with their being cared for, made good for hunting and being used as gardens by the local Kaurna people.

Kensington Gardens Reserve is due north and five blocks away. It is, along with Hazelwood Park (due west and five blocks away), one of our regular walking sites. We drive there these days; the dog is slowing down and it can be excruciating to walk those last few blocks home at a snail's pace after examining every fallen branch, all the edges of the duck pond, and the infinite potential of the playground for crumbs.

There are some wonderful trees in both parks including huge very old eucalyptus trees with strong presences. In the morning the dog and I walk quietly into their healing scent. It is not hard to imagine these suburbs without the houses, roads, shops and electricity wires. Near Kensington Park Oval, where Donald Bradman used to play cricket and once got more than 300 runs in one afternoon, is a quiet installation. The writing on metal strips runs along a set of low concrete steps on the edge of the park near the road. Each strip tells a story from the past about this place. One says: 'We the surviving Kaurna must walk these spirit lands for our cultural strength.' I often think about what this means, and whether thoughtful walking by anyone might be a good way of getting to know these spirit lands.

SEPTEMBER
walking it out

An essay is a walk, an excursion ... Everything is permitted — everything except the intentions of surveyors, farmers, speculators.

Michael Hamburger

Flying from Canada to New York involved entering the USA at the airport in Ottawa in a fairly casual way. Apart from American flags the desk where I submitted my passport included a small Statue of Liberty. Then I boarded a Canadian-made *Bombardier*, one of the smallest planes I have flown in. In the back row, in seat 13C, I watched over the toilet door for everyone. When an Indian man travelling with his mother, wife and two children got up to use it, his mother stole his seat. He then sat in her seat, and gave her an amazingly radiant smile.

Walking in New York was about various surprises. You think you know it from TV or movies but the reality is unexpected. The age of the city for one, its almost concave flatness, and the large numbers of black people who don't tend to show up in most movies. I saw many of them begging on the street, or hanging out near Penn Station with wheeled suitcases. It is clever because they look like travellers and have somewhere to keep their stuff. And you have to be open-eyed to see they are just standing there all day, not going anywhere.

Then there was the moistness of the air, the softness of the colours of the buildings. And a sense of fragility. And big though this city is, it is not phenomenally big the way things are in China.

All the bits of North America that I saw between the airport and Manhattan, in Brooklyn, in Chelsea and later on up in The Hamptons seemed old, very old. Not ancient-old or Renaissance-old, but old like a beach house, worn and old-fashioned. And all the air in New York City, surrounded as it is by seawater and therefore full of moisture, seemed bathed in old light and dust. When I walked around I looked down the streets through the passages between buildings to see tangible air, which is to say it was tinted in delicate yellows, browns, whites and blues, so it seemed left over from another time.

Wherever I went reminded me of Brian Eno's artwork *Mistaken Memories of Medieval Manhattan*. This video that I had seen at the 1982 *Sydney Biennale: Vision in Disbelief* was absorbing and haunting. It seemed to place a hand on my arm and say stay here, stop moving for a while. It showed the light coming and going on a view of the city and the sky from a window to slow ambient music that arrested time and slowed my breathing. The colours were rust and verdigris, while misty white air and clouds slowly unfurled above buildings.

Another memorable echo of a work seen at a Sydney Biennale struck me at the Metropolitan Museum of Art in New York. On Cockatoo Island in Sydney Harbour during the 2012 *Sydney Biennale: all our relations* I encountered *They Shimmer Still* a work by Imran Qureshi in what I consider is the best possible way to encounter art, by surprise. I discovered it as if it had never been seen before. I wandered along after getting off the ferry and finding my bearings I looked across and saw the concrete stairs and foundations of a demolished house. It appeared as if they had been splattered with blood which had then turned into flames, leaves, petal-like designs. Thus the work held formality and rawness, pattern and chaos coming together. Seeing it was like entering a dream. The red paint could have been metamorphosed blood from an old battle. It memorialised and made lyrical some undefined violence.

A painter trained in Pakistan as a traditional miniaturist Qureshi has taken elements of that careful and exquisite decorative historic style and expanded them onto large architectural surfaces, thus both loosening and rupturing the tradition. The work joins the sereneness of encountering an enclosed and ordered culture with the upheaval of its rules and certainties being splattered with violence and change. Or more simply with the aftermath of massacres and brutalities. It tells a story from history and intensely connects painting to the world rather than separating it.

A year later when I visited the roof garden of the Metropolitan Museum there on the ground beneath my feet were similar paintings by Qureshi. A wall sign included words from the artist explaining that he was responding to bombings in Lahore. 'Yes, these forms stem from the effects of violence. They are mingled with the colour of blood, but, at the same time, this is where a dialogue with life, with new beginnings, and fresh hope starts.'

Of course I know that the reality of all places is always smaller, softer, more ordinary and vulnerable than in your imagination. The walls of the Forbidden City in Beijing, for example, are peeling and patched, and washed in the sort of faded pink-red paint often used in Australia and New Zealand in the past on corrugated-iron sheds and tanks. Iron oxide, a red from the earth, echoes the red in our blood. And it makes the walls seem insubstantial, mortal, transient, in spite of all the history they have witnessed.

Alone in New York I felt nervous, then gradually relaxed. I went into Macy's and travelled to the top floor on an ancient narrow wooden escalator. The people working in the shop all looked at my feet. I went to all the usual places – the Strand Bookstore, the New Museum, the Guggenheim, the Whitney, the Metropolitan Museum of Art, MOMA, and many other less well-known places. I walked and walked until my old red sandals actually fell off my feet and I had to buy new ones in a shop full of nothing but shoeboxes and salespeople. I walked until my thighs were chafed, my feet were sore and my ankles swollen. It was hot and I suffered gastric emergencies. Though I like to walk because then I feel independent, eventually I caught a few buses, acknowledging that however flat the city is, the distances are significant. And that you see quite a lot from a bus that you miss on foot.

One of the first pilgrimages I walked in New York was to *The Earth Room*. I had in mind that the scent of this strange artwork by Walter De Maria would be a big feature of it. The work's combination of earth and interior space joins the dark bitterness and energy of soil to the enclosed peace of a room.

Both the longevity of the work and its simplicity appealed to me. Putting the two words 'earth' and 'room' together, and then literally putting the two things together, has a simple logic and makes a vivid mental image, even if you never make the journey to see it. The mystery and silence of a room in a big city filled up with earth, and kept as it was when first put together in 1977.

Not hard to find at its address 141 Wooster Street, Soho, *The Earth Room* is actually several adjoining rooms holding dark-brown soil, with practically no scent. Or that is what it was like when I was there. You find the door, you go up some stairs, a young invigilator sits in a small office nearby. Out of his sight you approach the door to *The Room* and its thigh-high glass barrier showing the depth of the soil. It is 22 inches/56 centimetres. There are 3600 square feet/335 square metres of floor space covered with 280,000 pounds/127,300 kilos of earth. You are asked to not touch or take photos. The piece was originally designed as a temporary exhibit and scheduled to close after three months. It's always closed in July and August – summertime. I guess it smells a lot then.

I ask is it watered? Is it cared for? Or does he just tell me? He says it is cared for, watered and raked once a week, by the same person who has been doing it since 1989. And it is the same earth. Yet rather than living soil or real earth with personality it looks like dark-brown potting mix. I have always thought of soil as full of life but after thirty-six years inside this lot has passed on. Surely there must be cockroaches and other life forms invading from outside. Suddenly the whole thing seems rather sterile – still wonderful as an idea, but lifeless as an experience. One for the imagination rather than the body.

They say it used to need weeding but now the soil is finally barren. I rather wish I had dropped in some rocket or prickly lettuce seeds, or simply a weed bomb from the southern hemisphere. Thinking here of cosmopolitan weeds not psychotropic ones. *The Earth Room* needs guerrilla gardeners.

I also thought about an artwork called *We should call it a living room*, made in Australia in 1975 by Aleks Danko, Joan Grounds, David Lourie and David Stewart. It's a time-lapse 16-mm film showing a room with a single lounge chair planted with seeds and watered. In a photo it looks almost like an underwater forest. It is about suburbia and entropy. I have never seen the film but I can see it in my mind's eye. Maybe it should be shown more often.

Walter De Maria made the first *Earth Room* in Munich in 1968 and another one at the Hessisches Landesmuseum in Darmstadt in 1974. Both were temporary. He is best known for another permanent artwork he made in a remote area of the high desert of western New Mexico called *The Lightning Field*. It consists of a one-mile-by-one-kilometre grid of 400 stainless-steel rods planted vertically in the ground. They change their appearance according to the time of day and weather, lighting up brilliantly during thunderstorms. And though they do not actually act as lightning rods, but evoke them, you can easily imagine it raging with lightning.

I visited *The Earth Room* on the twelfth anniversary of 9/11, not long after Walter De Maria died while attending his mother's 100th birthday celebrations. I came away from the *Room* wondering how on earth did he make a living?

Another day I walked to the Brooklyn Museum. At the time I was staying in Lafayette Street in Brooklyn renting a room in the brownstone terrace house of Waldemar, a West Indian man who had lost his stock exchange job on Wall Street in the Global Financial Crisis of 2008 (that great opportunity to rethink everything that only turned into a reboot, by which I mean disaster for most and a firmer grip on everything for the One Percent). Everyone I met in New York mentioned the GFC. Waldemar liked to watch sport on TV, rented out three rooms in his house, lived in the basement and spent a lot of time at home. The kitchen was full of tiny moths in flight.

I had a bedroom with an ensuite up a narrow flight of wooden stairs. My room had a fireplace with a mantelpiece and a wooden landing out into a backyard of big old trees held in common with other houses. Waldemar's wardrobe, overflowing with suits and shirts, was in my room behind a curtain. Brooklyn was full of trees, big old ones, lots of them ginkgos, and also many lively squirrels, with rapid almost electric movements and vibrating tails. Apart from the occasional siren the sound of Brooklyn was the rustle of wind in the trees like the sea.

In walking distance was the Brooklyn Museum, one of the oldest and largest art museums in the United States. It grew from a workingman's library in 1823 (that once employed Walt Whitman), to a grand edifice never quite completed to its full plan. Still it is big enough, and has the typical neo-classical Western Imperialism imitation-Greek façade of white pillars and statues, and the names of ancient Greeks, such as Plato and Sappho, and many other people that no one has ever heard of carved into the stone on the front of the building.

The Museum's Elizabeth A. Sackler Centre for Feminist Art contains a purpose-built glass room containing Judy Chicago's famous 1979 *Dinner Party* artwork, a huge ceremonial triangular table at which places are set for thirty-nine great women. Each table setting has a ceramic plate decorated with a creative interpretation of a woman's vulva. This type of imagery was once called 'central core', and was supposed to suggest an essential way of looking at the world as influenced by your sexual organs. It feels dated and mistaken. Recently I learned that the late Australian artist Frances Phoenix, who worked as a volunteer on the *Dinner Party*, actually embedded within it a criticism of the way the work was organised. She made an embroidery of the words 'no goddesses, no mistresses', a feminist version of the anarchist slogan 'no gods, no masters'. It was secretly sewn inside the work but Chicago found out and had it removed.

The US has a long long way to go in coming to terms with its indigenous cultures, with its African, Caribbean, Spanish and all the other cultures co-existing there. Or so it seems. This is clearly a large part of the mission of the Brooklyn Museum, though reconfiguring the entire notion of what a museum does is also on the cards. Here I saw a few contemporary artworks aiming to redress history. There was Sanford Biggers' *Blossom*, a large fake Bodhi tree merged with a grand piano playing the song 'Strange Fruit' by Billie Holiday. There was Fred Wilson's *Iago's Mirror*, made for him in Venice by glass artisans and backed with black instead of silver. And in another gallery, mishmashing the entire world together, there was a collection of disparate objects including a soul container from Bijagos, and a mesmerising film about African masks and Dutch wax fabric. Australia was present on a very old map and, elsewhere in the Museum, in a borrowed 1987 untitled painting by Western Desert Papunya Tula painter Yala Yala Gibbs Tjungurrayi.

The decorative arts collection of the Museum includes twenty-three American period rooms, ranging from the 17th to the 20th century. These curious rooms feel muffled and stunted, familiar and awkward. I am used to seeing the paraphernalia of indigenous lives in museums but to see these rooms twists my expectations out of order. These ones seemed especially full of sadness and constrained lives. Somehow it is the social deaths experienced in these spaces that come across. Is this my imagination, and I have read too many novels, or is there really a sense of embattlement in the furniture, the walls, the crockery? Brooklyn was once called Keskateuw and inhabited by the Canarsie, one of thirteen Algonquin tribes who had lived there for thousands of years. Maybe their ghosts are brooding in these rooms. The anthropology of whiteness sure needs a lot of filling out.

Another day I took the subway from Brooklyn (on Long Island) to Manhattan Island, its name is said to come from the Lenape language, meaning 'island of many hills'. I got off near Central Park where an ice cream kiosk was festooned with bananas, two of which I bought and ate immediately. Then, curious to see the famous displays put there in the thirties by anthropologist Franz Boas, I went to the Natural History Museum, situated west of Central Park. I expected them to be updated or bracketed by current information in a postcolonial kind of way but this was not the case. Thus the visit was like travelling back in time in thought, as well as in the flesh. It means that this part of the Natural History Museum is a museum of a museum, which is to say that it has not been shifted into the present but exists as an ideological space of the past. This is alarming; I thought things had moved on or opened up. As it turns out I was not the only person thinking this and three years after my visit a project to work on updating, conserving, restoring and enriching displays in the Northwest Coast Hall of Native American culture was begun. It includes working with First Nations people, and is to be revealed in 2020 on the 150th anniversary of the Museum.

You enter the Northwest Coast Hall as if it is an airlock through heavy swishing glass and wooden doors. The first diorama you see shows the Lenape, walking on Broadway, that strange bent street that cuts through the city of New York at a walking angle, in great contrast to the formal grid of the numbered streets. Clearly it is based on a Lenape walking trail. The diorama shows the Indians holding beads. The white men they are meeting hold guns and look cranky.

At another place in the Museum the explanation at the start of the Amazon Indian display says: 'Their traditions did not help them adjust to modern life' – a cool way of skimming over history.

Every country that is not Europe or America is in the Human Culture section of the Museum – Japan, China, South America and so on, on and on into galleries that seem to stretch forever.

Australia is tucked into Oceania, not far from a great cast of a Rapa Nui (Easter Island) moai statue worn smooth from people posing with it. The Oceania section was arranged by Margaret Mead starting in 1926 and remains undisturbed, thus maintaining a particular approach to knowledge alongside the persistent and insistent sensation of rambling in a random collection of objects.

Australia is present in a few glass cases containing a map, shields and wooden figures, some very good bark paintings collected by Catherine and Ronald Berndt in Arnhem Land in the 1950s and a photograph of a painted-up Aboriginal man waiting to be served at a shop selling $1 coffees. Its label says: 'At a railroad station in Sydney, an Aboriginal man in ceremonial dress waits for his train.' I guess he had been busking at Circular Quay. We learn that Australia is almost as big as the USA and that humans have inhabited it for more than 20,000 years.

On another pilgrimage I went to El Museo del Barrio, the 'Museum of the Neighbourhood' for the Latin American and Caribbean cultures of the US. On the outside of the building are the words 'A museum is a school: The artist learns to communicate: The public learns to make connections'. Here there was a clear sense of less financial resources than in other New York museums – and less audience. In their seventh biennial, *Here is where we Jump!*, I saw works by Pavel Acosta, who makes all-white images of famous paintings titled *Stolen paintings* using paint chips gathered from walls and the street. This practice originated from his art school years in Cuba, where art materials were scarce. I also saw works by Ramon Miranda Beltram, who transfers newspaper images of racial violence to concrete blocks thus making them seem like aged artefacts of another time, and by Ignacio Gonzalez-Lang who showed a Klu Klux Klan costume embroidered all over with colourful Native American patterns – and many others. I had a conversation with a museum guard (practically all museum guards I saw in the US and Canada were black) who told me that he was promoting the careers of other people, in music, to make them seem brighter by providing an inky blackness behind their light. I said it sounded good and he looked really pleased.

On my very last day in New York I travelled by train from one end of the city to the other, from Fort Tryon Park in the north to Battery Park in the south. It turned out to be a day stolen from time due to a miscalculation of my departure date. I had buried my phone in my bag while out so it wasn't until I arrived back at the loft apartment after 6 pm, balancing a pizza and some beers, that my landlord managed to tell me that he had been trying to reach me most of the day. Someone else was due to move in to my room for a night before flying off to a wedding. My landlord Emanuel offered me his sofa and TV room for one night for $100 so I quickly packed my stuff and moved across. It was almost as if I had planned it.

Earlier in the day I had happily wandered with that particular freedom that comes over me when I am travelling and know that I will soon be leaving a place. And then I wonder why I don't feel like that every day.

It takes about an hour on the train from the centre of the city to Fort Tryon Park where The Cloisters, a museum of medieval art, an offshoot of the Metropolitan Museum of Art, is located on a hill overlooking the Hudson River. The Cloisters incorporates four cloisters from medieval France, a chapel from Spain, and multiple other items of European history including stone carvings, illuminated books and tapestries.

Once you alight from the train it is still necessary to walk for about ten minutes to get to The Cloisters and in so doing you look out over the river and see the cliffs called the New Jersey Palisades, and thus how close the edges of New York City are to wildlife and places apparently completely empty of people. It is a little like being in Sydney on a ferry and seeing the edges of the harbour coming down to the water and somehow knowing they have been just like that for thousands of years.

In Australia, cloisters are generally found in universities. I always find something calming in their sense of enclosure and quiet encouragement of walking, of meditation and conversation. They evoke Plato's Academy under the olive trees; they possess the consolation of shelter, the importance of spaces dedicated to talking, listening, contemplation and reverie. My father told me firmly to avoid universities, even though he worked at them for many years – or was it because he worked at them? I see his point, yet I know in some way, it is at universities, lost in words and thinking, where some of my people are located. They are also in museums and gardens and libraries, while others are walking on the beach.

The medieval gardens of The Cloisters were the loveliest part of my visit. Looking at the garden plots with their wicker trellises, the trees and herbs with their labels, plus a fabulous black, blue and yellow butterfly, evoked the joy of my own garden and the peaceful lost hours I spend in it, hiding from everything in the company of the quiet lives of the plants, their familiar leaves and the birds.

Another delightful surprise was that my visit coincided with the first time a contemporary artwork was presented in The Cloisters. *The Forty Part Motet*, by Janet Cardiff, was a sound installation in the Fuentidueña Chapel. Arranged in a large oval around the walls of the chapel were forty simple black

SEPTEMBER – walking it out

speakers on stands playing an eleven-minute reworking of the Elizabethan choral work *Spem in alium numquam habui* (*In No Other Is My Hope*) by Thomas Tallis. Each speaker represented a voice in the Salisbury Cathedral Choir, which included children and amateur performers.

The singing drew me in from a distance and it was free to enter. It was possible to walk, sit or stand still among the speakers, feel the singing vibrate through your ears and in your body and be infused by it for as long as you wanted. An unexpected and very effective part of the work was hearing the singers quietly talking to one another in the gap between the end and the beginning of the singing. It was as if they were, though invisible, actually there, excited and present in the transformation that happened when they all sang together. And then for the eleven minutes of singing you could feel your heart moving in your body, and just be.

The significance of music crosses cultures. Yolŋu leader and artist Djambawa Marawili said:

> *The land is complete. It has all that it needs for its continuation and sustenance. But it cannot express itself. It cannot sing, paint and dance its identity. And so it has grown a tongue. That tongue is the Yolŋu. The Indigenous people of Australia. They exist to articulate the land. That is their reason for existence.*

If that is true then surely it applies to all people who live on the earth.

In the short story *The clear voice suddenly singing*, Australian author Amanda Lohrey quotes from ethnomusicologist Marius Schneider: 'Singing calls creation into existence and then sustains it. All songs are about the hunger for and affirmation of life.' And from otolaryngologist and inventor Albert Tomatis: 'When you are singing it is the universe that speaks and we are the machines to translate the universe.'

Right down at the south end of the island of Manhattan is Battery Park, which gets its name from the fact that the Dutch colonisers had their fortification and artillery there. Looking out from there you see mostly the sea and the sky, both vast and gray that particular day, and the Statue of Liberty standing greenly out on the water and on the horizon to her right the striped and spired building on Ellis Island where migrants including my paternal grandparents were once processed.

Nearby was my destination, the George Gustav Heye Centre, the New York branch of the National Museum of the American Indian, located in the old Custom House that also houses the New York Archives and Bankruptcy Court. In 1897 Heye, whose German immigrant father made a fortune in petrol, started avidly collecting pieces of North and South American indigenous culture, an obsession he continued for more than 45 years.

The Centre's permanent exhibition, *Infinity of Nations*, said to be a phrase first used by French missionaries encountering the peoples of the Americas, displays objects of all kinds in glass cases. Words for 'home' and 'belonging' from each different nation are written on the glass with their translations creating a sense of multiple voices and ways of being. As well as loss and retrieval. The museum was almost empty but full of ghosts.

> *numin wetes*
> 'our land'
> NIMI'IPUU
>
> *oyate tamakoce*
> 'land of the people'
> LAKOTA

SEPTEMBER – walking it out

pachamama/apu
'mother earth/father mountain'
QUECHUA

gaa-zaaga eganikaag
'The land of many lakes'
OJIBWE

inuvik
'the place of man'
INUIT

sa'aqtik'oy
'it is sheltered from the wind'
CHUMASU

pahee kushke ethe wah
'where the sawgrass is'
MICCOSUKEE SEMINOLE

paba hanokwaetu
'a vast ragged place'
NORTHERN PAIUTE

tsee ee chi
'red rock'
MECSCALERO APACHE

tei yurienaka matiniere
'place of our mother'
WIXARIKA

lum, luum, kad
'earth'
MAYA

> *choyumpelu ketran*
> 'the one where seeds sprout'
> MAPUCHE
>
> *pachamama*
> 'mother earth and light of the sun'
> AYMARA

The Museum of the American Indian felt very quiet though in the gift shop the woman told me how successful their Jimi Hendrix exhibition had been. In the foyer near the water fountain a sign said: 'The water is out of order in the Museum of the American Indian', which reminded me ineluctably of Allen Ginsberg.

High up on the façade of another customhouse nearby were the names of trading cities on fancy shield forms and there, alongside Rio De Janeiro, Buenos Aires, Naples, Genoa, Gibraltar, Paris, Cherbourg and Sydney, was my home city Adelaide.

Thinking of home I went into a nearby delicatessen for tea and a ham roll before wandering around. The park on the seaside edge of Battery Park was being dug up, its trees hung with orange plastic bunting to protect them and here, on an awning surrounding the redevelopment of the waterfront area, was printed a long sentence, which I recognised as the words from very near the end of *The Great Gatsby* where F. Scott Fitzgerald imagines the Dutch arriving.

> *... for a transitory enchanted moment man must have held his breath in the presence of this continent, compelled into an aesthetic contemplation he neither understood nor desired, face to face for the last time in history with something commensurate to his capacity for wonder.*

And I walked down to the very edge of the island, sat for a while and took a few notes and photos, but the park was covered in rubbish and felt abandoned.

The dog sleeps a lot, mostly in complete, deep and somehow comforting silence, but he does have a register of snores as well: grunty, whistly, squeaky, fluty, groany. He does a lot with his breath to communicate in general. He has faith that a deep breath or faint lip-smacking movement outside the front door will be heard and he will be let in. If it isn't he might give one woof or a tiny strange yelp. When you hug him sometimes he makes a nice *grrr* noise deep in his chest.

The apparent simplicity of his life sometimes makes me feel complicated and agitated. The place I call home is very like a midden, a place where people have lived and eaten, an almost geological space where things rise to the surface and are found with other objects in strange combinations. Scratching through them reveals how much has been forgotten, how much can be remembered, and how much is lost forever. And it is astonishing how often the vital lost or unknown 'thing' is found at the right moment.

OCTOBER
the quiet dark

*The thought lost
in the eyes of a unicorn
appears again
in a dog's laugh*

Vladimir Holan

I arrived in Prague by train from Linz through woodpiles and allotments and meadows with yellow butterflies drifting over them. I saw birch tree forests; fields of canola, corn, and potatoes; rosehips, apples, great swathes of yarrow and white swans; a woman with chickens; two old men, a child and a dog standing by a river; people walking in single file on paths through fields; a dog on a small balcony. All the train station buildings were painted a particular yellow. And as we approached the city there was a scrawling of graffiti saying NO CULTURE NO LIFE. There was no way of knowing if it was a description or a manifesto.

Seeing fenced allotments with their tiny huts, neat rows of vegetables and fruit trees, sun-umbrellas and chairs always makes me dream about a tiny personal paradise, a productive garden, a sanctuary, a small section of the earth that is yours to design and tend.

OCTOBER – the quiet dark

The train trip was so slow I thought maybe I was reading a Russian novel, or going back in time through a wormhole. At some point the train stopped and we all had to get off and walk over and across the tracks with our luggage, pile onto a bus to Veselí nad Lužnicí then board another train. No platform, no explanation, no assistance, no loud announcements, no technology. Luckily a Russian woman sitting in my carriage, a travel agent whose daughter was studying in Prague, helped me out. Then she insisted on buying me a half-hour public transport ticket when we arrived.

Once in Prague my first task was to go to the Shakespeare and Sons second-hand English bookshop on one side of the river and get the key to my apartment on the other side. After getting the key and buying a David Sedaris book I caught the tram and managed to get help from the other people on it, through eye contact and gestures, about where to alight. Later in the day, in the famous Wenceslas Square that is not a square, I saw buskers standing around with exotic birds. One was a sulphur-crested cockatoo from Australia. The people look so pleased with themselves, not just that but so blessed and thrilled by the beauty and vitality of the bird, that I didn't go too near for fear I should tell them off.

Next day I went to the Veletrzni Palace, the National Gallery, where art not of Czech origin is called foreign art. In contrast Australian galleries designate art not made by Australians to be international art. A wall sign in the Veletrzni promises that the story of modern and contemporary art seen here is different from that conveyed by other world museums. An example of this is that motorbikes and cameras, china and glass, typewriters and radios are displayed in with the art. Thus art and design, life and art, a sense of elegance and the everyday, are brought together. Thought-provoking design is a striking and pervasive element in this city; I stopped again and again to appreciate the chairs in cafés, waiting rooms, restaurants.

I learnt from the doors in the Gallery the words for push (*tam*) and pull (*sem*), and from a sign taped to a kinetic work the word for defect (*porucha*) and beware (*pozor*). Later I went into a hardware shop and bought a sign saying *pozor pes* (beware dog) for my front door at home. Walking through the many galleries I saw the obligatory Rodin, a Beuys *Intuition* box, and many Czech paintings of the forties, fifties, and sixties that looked roughly similar to Australian paintings of the same time, though I had never heard of the artists. What does it mean? The principle of resemblance, the repetition of influence, something about the way thought echoes? Definitely something about world art being more, much more, than we generally know.

There were three fragments of film showing Alphonse Mucha, one of the most well-known Czech painters. One where he walks around a corner in white shoes and waves, one where he nods his head, and one where he is sitting in front of a huge painting. Among contemporary works I was especially entertained by Milena Dopitová's video *Sixtysomething*, which shows the artist and her sister being made up, greyed up and dressed up to look as if they are over sixty. Then they dance together. It is solemn, sad and hilarious.

Here in the café, the sole visitor, I ordered tea and cake. It took a while to come. The man running the café told me that he had revived an old machine with a magnetic stirrer from a chemical factory. He was using it to making cordial and soft drinks. He told me how enjoyable it was to work in the café and suggested that it was as good a place as any to be.

Next I took a bus to the DOX Centre for Contemporary Art where a huge red skull on a crane was hanging over the rooftop café, but they were between exhibitions. A mural on the wall near the entrance in both Czech and English consisted of words signed by the political art collective Pode Bal.

> *I am a Czech coward,*
> *who looked on*
> *when they loaded the jews,*
> *hailed the Nazis,*
> *waved to the communists*
> *and then wanted*
> *the security of a tenfold.*

A friend with knowledge of Czech has explained this awkward last line as meaning 'complete security'. The Pode Bal online catalogue explains further: ' "Security of a tenfold" was a popular slogan of one of the privatization campaigns resulting in massive "tunnelling" (asset stripping of public trust funds in the early 1990s in the Czech Republic).' Founded in 1997, Pode Bal have made many works drawing attention to local themes, such as the links between the new ruling elite and the collaborators of the former secret police; the eviction of ethnic Germans after World War Two and the seizing of their property; and anti-drug legislation. They also critique art institutions. They believe in 'reviving the cognitive and therapeutic functions of art, that solidarity and resistance are possible, and that art does matter'. I haven't met them but we are on the same page.

My two visits to Prague were focused on going to museums, as many as I could – though following the advice of my Czech cousin David Radok, not to the Museum of Communism, situated above McDonald's in Wenceslas Square, nor the KGB Museum or the Kafka Museum (well I did enter the shop looking for a souvenir). My own private Kafka experience occurred in my very high-ceilinged rented apartment located near a cemetery with a view of a futuristic church and many empty and desolate-looking apartments across the way. Here I was woken at night by a drunk moving noisily along the street and then saw the shadow of a giant cockroach waving its antennae on the ceiling. Or was I dreaming? I can easily imagine a projection of this metamorphic creature as a secret artwork, quietly existing somewhere in the city and being seen from time to time – more an urban legend than real.

Before visiting Prague I had made plans to meet up with David. We had met in Czechoslovakia as children about fifty years earlier. I remembered elements of that visit, even though I was uncertain of our exact familial relationship, as was he.

The first question he asked was 'Who are you?' when we met as arranged on the first floor of Café Louvre in the centre of Prague. Luckily when I described my father he remembered meeting him several times and that as a child he used to call him 'the shouting man'. We worked on it and it turns out that our great-grandfathers were brothers. Mine left the village to go to secondary school then studied mechanical engineering in Prague, worked in Berlin and later settled in Koenigsberg in East Prussia where he became the head of the Union Foundry building ships and trains; David's stayed on in the village working in the family business as a merchant. There is a studio photograph of the three brothers Elias, Bernhard and Max sitting around a table. My grandfather Fritz is there too as a child in knickerbockers, and his older brother Reinhold. They all look Jewish and the men have big dark beards. The Radoks in Koenigsberg were naturalised in 1895 and Elias changed his name to Emil in 1902, as well as having the family christened. I have some engineer's drawings that he made in fine black ink given to me by my father as well as a notebook full of diagrams.

On my second longer trip to Prague I stayed in David's

elegant apartment, had many meals with him and his partner, including a coffee named after him in his local café, visited a lot more museums and saw a few solo exhibitions by Czech artists. The documentary photographer Viktor Kolář had a large retrospective exhibition at one of the sites of the Prague City Gallery called The Stone Bell, an early Gothic building where it is said Charles IV, Holy Roman Emperor and King of Bohemia, was probably born. This convoluted building is full of surprising corners, painted beams and stairs.

Some few photographs, whether taken by your mother, father, friend, you or a famous photographer, have a curious tickling tendency to lodge in your brain. *Everlasting encounter of gypsy man with horse,* one of Kolář's most famous photographs (that I immediately recognised), is of a man looking at a horse. The horse whose tail has been cut very short stands in a corner flush against a wall facing a roller door. The man has his back to the viewer and his hands on his hips. It appears that the horse is being judged or put on trial by the man, if you look closely there are objects lined up near its feet as if it is being trained to stand in a very narrow space.

The story of Viktor Kolář is embedded in the history of the Czech Republic and the waxing and waning of freedom and surveillance in it. Most of his photographs are of the grim coalmining town of Ostrava, its inhabitants and surroundings. He took on recording this specific place early in his life as a documentary project to which he dedicated most of his work. In an interview Kolář said his aim was: 'To photograph someone with a common face as though he were the centre of the universe.'

In 1968 after the invasion by the Soviet Union Kolář left Czechoslovakia to live in Canada but even though he was quite successful there he decided to return in 1973, knowing he would face political reprisal. Because of homesickness, because of loneliness, and surely because of his commitment to Ostrava, he went home.

Another Czech artist whose solo show I happened upon by chance was Jan Křížek, whose substantial retrospective exhibition *Jan Křížek (1919–1985) and the artistic Paris of the 50s* was on at the Waldstein Riding School. It contained his artwork as well as works by artists he worked alongside in Paris, such as Jean Dubuffet and Pablo Picasso. And Art Brut by Miguel Hernandez and Henri Salingardes. And even an Adolf Wölfli from 1930 called *Christopher Columbus*, with terrific staring vivid eyes.

Křížek was the first to show his work in Dubuffet's Foyer de l'Art Brut in Paris in 1947. His work is raw, rough, alive, intense, and often focuses on the human figure. Some of his small watercolour paintings of patterns are like fragments of textiles, a wooden carved work from 1947 resembled a printing block for fabric, other works were on used aged cardboard, or looked like used aged cardboard. His carved sculptures in stone and wood echo Cycladic sculpture. The work of Paul Gauguin, Amedeo Modigliani, Henri Gaudier-Brzeska, Danila Vassilieff and early Jacob Epstein also came to mind. Křížek was an artist bordering on being an outsider, though he was not isolated from society by illness like many outsider artists.

In 1962, at the age of forty-four, Křížek stopped making art with the conviction, in his words, that he had 'solved his problem' and instead turned to raising bees in the French countryside where he was living. In the documentary film *Jan Křížek, Sculpture and Bees*, made in 2005 by Martin Řezníček and shown in the exhibition, Křížek's widow, whose face we never see, recalls their life together while domestic details of their simple home that he built and the trees and fields of the surrounding countryside are shown. The film is mesmerising, hypnotic in its indirectness, in its showing of artworks, of a devoted relationship, of a domestic and working space, a garden, the life of an artist, beehives. It is said that Krížek's work is almost forgotten. The film points at the value of his life, even though few know much about it. An eloquent subtext here was the material poverty in which he and wife lived while he focused on making his work, on solving his problem.

Then I visited the Czech Museum of Ethnography. Called Musaion, rather than the Czech word Muzeum, it sounds quite Greek (and more like 'Mouseion', the name of the man who may have given his name to the first museum). I got off the tram, walking slowly on the cobblestones in the rain with my borrowed umbrella, up the hill through the damp garden and into the almost empty galleries. But rather than being a museum of exotic 'other than Czech' cultures (which was what I expected from the word 'ethnography') it displayed the traditional Czech folk cultures of Bohemia, Silesia and Moravia and was full of objects and stories from the everyday life of rural communities in the 18th, 19th and the first half of the 20th century.

A rough wooden angel from the collection is the symbol of the museum. It is in many ways a place of elegy, as the everyday ordinary past, the diversity between regions, the common ground of daily life and regular festivals and feasts drifts into history. Masks and costumes, tableaux, toys and stories were juxtaposed in glass cases, making the past seem both precious and petrified. Such social history is often presented through stories about food and its preparation. It is a common ground of which we know the elements. Thus a rack of knives and a great model of a pig's head were presented alongside information about potatoes and cabbages. In a model kitchen the sacredness of the kitchen table and the stove were emphasised. The corner diagonal from the oven was the Sacred Corner or Sacred Nook. The kitchen table could never be sold or given away, beaten or sat upon.

In yet another Museum that was a temporary resting-place as the National Museum at the top of Wenceslas Square was closed were some signs for children making games from history that shocked me with their grimness. Among the displays of old toys, crockery, photographs, books, desks and jewellery I read: 'Your father has spent all his money and property on drink or lost it in card games. You move to a small and murky flat.' And alongside a tray of dried legumes: 'Common corporal punishment was kneeling on peas or small logs. How long will you manage?'

I also went to the Náprstek Museum of Asian, African and American Cultures where the exotic 'other than Czechs' were to be found. Starting in 1862, and based on a private collection, the Náprstek began as a collection of cultural donations from expatriate Czechs. Here it was the presentation that reflected strongly on their location in Prague. In the entrance hall maps were painted on both the walls and beneath a sweeping staircase; Australia sitting up in a corner above the mezzanine. The elegant wooden-edged glass cases in which artefacts were arranged boasted astonishing sweeping curves. The Pacific was present in many objects and eloquent sheets of bark cloth painted in black and brown as well as unpainted ones arranged around the walls of a circular room.

On the other side of the river was the Kampa Museum of modern and contemporary art based in old flour mill buildings on Kampa Island. Most of the works on show in its many galleries are from the private collection of Jan and Meda Mládek their motto being 'If a nation's culture survives, then so too does the nation'. Again, as in the Veletrzni, many works by

Czech artists I didn't know were intermingled with works by foreign artists thus opening new chapters of art history.

Later I found out that the poet Vladimir Holan, whom I first read in the seventies, ended his life in reclusive poverty on this island. His book was one volume of the Penguin Modern European Poets that I bought from the Union Bookshop at the University of Adelaide in the early seventies for ninety-nine cents and, like those by Zbigniew Herbert and Apollinaire, remains a close companion. Each brought a breath of Europe to the hot dry streets of Adelaide.

The Jewish cemetery in Prague is closely packed with gravestones, like a mouth overfull with teeth. Here among many others lie the remains of Rabbi Loew, who made the most famous golem in the late 16th century to defend the Jewish ghetto in Prague. A golem is made from clay and is a sort of automaton or robot (the word 'robot' has a Czech origin too, as does dalek). It is somehow both helpless and very strong – like a mute Frankenstein. Most golem, like Wandjina from the Kimberley, don't have mouths. It is also said that the story of the golem was a German invention, but that perhaps it came originally from a Jewish oral story. Curiously the Jewish cemetery in Prague was not destroyed by the Nazis. I read somewhere that this was because Hitler was afraid of the golem – or did I imagine that?

The Nazis brought Jewish artefacts from synagogues across Europe to Prague. They planned to make a Jewish museum there, to be called the 'Exotic Museum of an Extinct Race'. I didn't go into the Jewish cemetery in Prague but looked down on it from the window of the nearby Museum of Decorative Arts while standing in a gallery full of huge glass vitrines stuffed full of marvellously intricate china and glass. Then I went to see the Czech Museum of Cubism where a 17th-century statue of the Black Madonna of Prague sits outside on the corner of the building behind a grid. But it was closed that year.

Even though he is a busy opera director working in both Sweden and Prague, David kindly found time to take me to visit Koloděje nad Lužnicí, the village that my paternal great-grandfather Elias left in 1858 to make his way in a bigger world. Its Jewish cemetery dates from the 17th and 18th centuries. David remembers hiding there to smoke cigarettes as a child. Like the one in Prague it is intact, though nowhere near as crowded. In long grass it contains gravestones with the names of a few of my ancestors upon them, including Aaron Radok, father of Elias. And the pairs of open hands carved on some of the old gravestones mean that those buried under them are from the priestly tribe of Aaron, older brother of Moses.

The Jews moved to Koloděje in the 13th century after being expelled from the nearby town of Moldautein (Tyn nad Vltavou) where they had been scapegoated because of the plague. In 1787 they had to take surnames, though the origin of the surname Radok remains something of a mystery as it is not on Kaiser Joseph's official list of possible surnames at the time and is considered neither Czech nor German.

The most famous people born in Koloděje were David's father Alfred and David's uncle Emil. A plaque with their names, dates and achievements sits on the wall of the house now owned by David, where they were born. Alfred was a much-acclaimed theatre director. He also made three films, *The Long Journey (Daleká cesta)* being the best and most well-known. Made in 1948 it was the first film in the world to deal with the Holocaust. Falling foul of the Communist government, which considered both expressionism and formalism to be subversive, it was then banned in the Czech Republic for the next forty years. When the Russians invaded Czechoslovakia in 1968, Alfred and his family left to live in Sweden.

Daleká cesta was influenced by Orson Welles' *Citizen Kane* (1941) and has been compared to it. An excerpt from *Daleká cesta* appears in Stanley Kubrick's *Clockwork Orange*. It was shot partly in Prague's Barrandov film studios and partly on location in the concentration camp and ghetto Theresienstadt/Terezín. This notorious camp was presented in Nazi propaganda as a model Jewish town but was really a total nightmare; more than 33,000 people died there and almost 60,000 were crowded into barracks designed for 7000 combat troops. It was a transit camp to Treblinka and Auschwitz.

Once back in Adelaide I ordered a subtitled DVD of *Daleká cesta*. It was posted in Ostrava. I watched it closely hoping to write down my response straightaway but instead simply set aside my notebook and watched. It memorably conveys the surreal disorienting nightmarish way that people's lives were confused, threatened and lost. There is a vivid moment emphasizing the crowding when the main character the Jewish doctor Hannah stands at the door of a room in the ghetto as more and more women enter, each looking for some space. Hannah's father has special shoes made to hide money and asks her for hair-dye in order to look younger; then there are the words over the entrance to the camp saying '*Arbeit macht frei*' (work sets you free). And the large yellow stars sewn on people's clothing and the big white numbers painted on their suitcases.

Alfred's father Viktor was fifty-seven years old and his grandfather Bernhard ninety-five when they both died in Terezín concentration camp, as did many other Radoks. A list of them and the dates and places of their deaths appears in a Czech book about Alfred that David showed me. Alfred was imprisoned in the last months of the war in the detention camp of Klettendorf near Wrocław, from which he managed to escape. Emil too managed to evade death.

Emil and Alfred both contributed to the invention of the nonverbal theatre called Laterna Magika that began as a Czech contribution to Expo 58, the first World's Fair held after World War Two in Brussels. Laterna Magika used the projection of images in new ways and was experimental in combining technology with live dance and theatre. These days, though Laterna Magika is based in the centre of Prague, it has become light tourist entertainment, commercialised and emptied of artistic exploration. The Laterna Magika building is famous for being the place where the Civic Forum headed by Vaclav Havel was based during the Velvet Revolution in 1989.

Emil, who studied art history, worked briefly as an art critic and editor in Prague, and then made notable works in Canada and America following on from the Laterna Magika experiments. He wasn't afraid of big topics. His two major works were *The Creation of the World* for Walt Disney's EPCOT Centre in 1982, and *The Taming of the Demons* for Vancouver's Expo '86, which contains a message about the taming of the demons of new communication systems. *The Creation of the World* concerns evolution from primal matter all the way to advanced technologies. Pre-digital but not pre-computer, both works used multiple cubes and projections, slide projectors, sound, and moving images to create immersive, spectacular and thought-provoking experiences. Emil was described by Jean-Claude Delorme, president of Teleglobe Canada, as 'probably in the area of audiovision what Marshall McLuhan was in literature'.

Koloděje is on the wide slow Lužnicí river in which I came very close to drowning as a child. David owns the substantial three-storey house on the river where his great-grandfather and grandfather once lived and ran their business. After 1968 it was taken over by the Communist government and used as a summerhouse but through the efforts of his mother was eventually returned to him.

There are two great storage buildings with green mossy roofs near the house as well as a glass-and-wood pergola. The house has large elegant rooms and a patio. I stayed there in 1962 with my sister, fearful I would never again see my parents, who had gone to the Soviet Union. This time I stayed a night in the same room we had shared and then spent a morning walking along the river, crossing the bridge, seeing a fisherman in a flat-bottomed boat, and photographing the forest nearby and the reflections on the water. All around is very green, very quiet, very overgrown, and the water is deep and moves slowly. And most surprising and wonderful of all, I saw many familiar herbs such as yarrow, tansy, comfrey, plantain, dock and dandelions growing wild and abundantly on the riverbanks. My ancestors here were not farmers and did not work the land but maybe the women collected medicinal herbs. And there must be herbalists and gardeners in my ancestry, as everywhere I go I study trees and plants as if they are part of my family; instinctively and insistently I collect seeds and cuttings. And it may mean something that the maiden name of Gladys, my maternal grandmother, was Gardiner.

Being in the Czech Republic was about experiencing a place where some of my people had lived. Now I really need to go to Ireland and Scotland. Looking for your people, like self-knowledge, is often not smooth or clear, neither satisfying nor conclusive. I wonder if there is too much emphasis on ancestors, if we can't find or don't know our ancestors are we lesser people? Do we belong to one piece of earth or to the whole planet?

The phrase 'the old country' is sometimes used by people in Australia to refer to the place their parents or grandparents – or even they – were born. It is often a recognition of having origins on the other side of the world, even if you have never been there. And it is a term full of emotion and energy, and often other languages and ways of being. The word 'country' is used by Aboriginal people in Australia to refer to their sense of belonging and attachment to a particular place as well as their knowledge of it, relationship to it, and responsibility for it – including all its living and non-living elements. Surely the feelings and experiences embedded in these concepts are not totally exclusive of each other but have something in common. And surely more and more we must all see ourselves as belonging to the earth and think about her welfare and that of all humans, plants and animals, not only about those who share our ethnic or cultural history. Because we are all related.

Legends surround the dog. The Hahndorf Interim Animal Shelter where I got him told me only that he was picked up wandering around Murray Bridge. I have two theories about this. One is that he was a stud (a lover) and a fighter. When he got old his star waned and they let him go. The other is that he lived with his grandmother until she died and then he fell on hard times. As he is missing a couple of teeth and has a scar on his ear I tend to think that the first story is the correct one. He has dusted up a few dogs since I have had him and would clearly never back down in a fight. He is also an explorer and scavenger. When he came to live with me he was thin and had a hoarse bark and spiky fur. Now he is well-covered with a beautiful glossy coat and a crisp loud bark. He smells like a warm mouse with a slight fishy undertone. Staffordshire Terriers are known for chatting, a canine version of talking, and when I come home after being out for a while I often get a good chat.

NOVEMBER
the dodo and the dappled garden

We wish to explore kindness the vast and peaceful country
Apollinaire

The daddy-long-leg spiders have just had a large family and I don't have the heart to kill them. They start so small, the big ones must be quite old.

The ants are in the kitchen but I have no plans to chemically wipe them out. In fact I follow their trail and open and place the old peanut butter jar at the far end of it. They are interested for a while but then go somewhere else. I too stopped eating it a while ago.

The birds are in the garden, watching me.

The possum/s is/are in the roof, pissing down the wall occasionally, but not every day nor in the same place every time, and I really should have it/them removed (though as everyone knows they always come back).

Possums are both regular and irregular in their habits and I like this; they are not machines. Things happen to them, they get electrocuted or run over, their bodies lie on the ground, their skulls gradually being revealed, their fur coming to look like a pile of mould around a chalky skeleton, a small dead puppet lost by the side of the road. They sleep in, they stay out, they maintain an irregular regularity, though whenever there are strange and sudden noises in the middle of the night, like a heavy piece of wood being dragged across the roof, a thumping chasing bumping sound or a giant foot hitting the wall it is certain to be a possum.

The moment I write about the irregularity of possum habits, a possum gives its throaty nighthorror *haaarrgh* right outside the window. It must be 9 pm. Sometimes I see one silhouetted against the sky on the roof or clambering over the solar panels and we freeze and stare at each other. There were even a few times when a mother and child in the Cootamundra wattle tree looked down at me. She had what looked like a black clown's mouth drawn under her pink nose. Recently I went outside in the evening and one was in the banksia tree eating flowers. We both froze but I spoke to it and it then stopped staring at me and went on with its night.

When you see a possum, as with many animals, you tilt your head back a little a few times and breathe in softly through your nose, this way you get their scent, or at least look as if you do. That is the movement they make when they look at you.

Haaarrgh. Haaarrgh. Haarrgh.

If you didn't know it was a possum you would swear there was someone doing a very good job of noisily dying in your ear or trying to frighten you. It could be a bunyip. Or the deep groaning cry of male koalas thinking about mating, which sound like six-foot-tall gorillas with huge swinging arms.

Very few chemicals are used in this house and garden, even to clean. It is a biozone – or biome – of soft homes for all, a quarter-acre block, a sanctuary in the suburbs, a shrubby garden, a sheltered workshop, a dusty house, a place where roots may be put down and get tangled up, where there is a vast and uncharted number of different overlapping territories or countries with different beings living in them. There are the rarely seen but very fierce inch ants living near the clothesline in a low-lying multi-storeyed clay cave (I give them a wide berth). There are the possums. There are skinks and geckos under pots and in crevices, there are lots of snails, and pigeons, crows, rosellas and rainbow lorikeets in the front garden, and there are magpies in the big blue gum trees watching over and patrolling the backyard. And the occasional blue-tongue lizard.

The more everything stays the same the more inhabitants there are: worms and black beetles, dragonflies, large ash-grey grasshoppers, cabbage moths, mottled geckos, praying mantises, aphids, pale-blue butterflies, flies, bees, crusader beetles, green leaf bugs, slaters, millipedes, swallowtail butterflies, spiders, earwigs, weevils, small squiggly things, cicadas, crickets, yellow butterflies, tiny tiny tiny bugs. You often need to sit still to see them, or lift up a stone or pot or trough. Often in summer I see a koala, slung over a tree in the heat, sharp claws hanging down, small amber eyes watching. They too are co-habitants.

When it was my mother's garden from the 1960s to the 1990s, it was low and flat. She called it a rock garden, planted it with rockery plants and dug in bags and bags of peat moss. She raked and fertilised, swept and pruned; and we all helped to scavenge and then lay down pieces of slate as rocks. I remember pushing a wheelbarrow piled with slate from a few streets away. The much older edges of the garden beds are made from pointy rocks from the nearby quarry. Here and there in the folds of the rocks clear quartz crystals flash.

In the few photos of people in the garden during those years there is a lot of space between their faces and the plants below them. Today the people are dwarfed by the plants that tower over and around them. This manifestation of the garden is full of dappled light. Places to hide. Places to stop. There are chairs and tables placed here and there. It is a beer garden, a sky-observing garden, a cocktail garden with a rough brick platform and an old washing-machine drum on it as a hearth where I cook on a fire sometimes. It is an outdoor studio garden, a sculpture garden, a herb, greens and flower garden. It is a wanderers' garden, a poverty garden, a garden of love and invisibility.

I began slowly adding fruit trees, first a quince in an out-of-the-way place behind the shed near the fence, then another one in the middle of the lawn, and a currant grape vine on the trellis near the clothesline. Then a rogue fig tree found growing by the side of the road that has never had anything but dry fruit. And a peach tree. I read that the Japanese say the reason to have a garden is to look after it.

I planted two European plum trees for my mother when she died and a Japanese one for my father. Since then I have planted many native plants as well as two apricots, three more grapevines, three figs, another peach, a dwarf nectarine, two more plum trees and many native plants. Just about everything else is grown from cuttings, mostly not given but broken off in passing, stolen branches of succulents, small dragon trees salvaged from under their parents, geraniums, strong tough plants, herbs, seeds, gathered wherever, country town, suburban garden, city walks. And a few that were gifts.

The summer garden is dry and full of air. In my thoughts I compare it again and again to a painted garden on a wall, a frescoed place of fanned blue-grey leaves, dark cypress towers, yellow, pink and white flowers, hanging fruit and birds hiding in trees or perching on the edges of birdbaths, of chalky skies and stones baked by heat, of dipping butterflies, silently slinking skinks and faint vanilla perfumes from herbs, mulch and unseen pollens.

It is a place you might walk into but prefer to dream into – like you do with a painting where you can slowly arrange your thoughts like flowers in a vase.

You can put your hand flat on a painted wall; you can lie down in front of it and place your feet into the garden. You can imagine the grittiness and flatness of the wall under your fingers at the same time as a sense of light, both expanding and somehow solid, enters your lungs, makes your concentration dissolve and drift into space. It connects you to the closeness of touch as well as to illimitable distance.

When I don't want to hurry, when I am enjoying stillness, a hot afternoon in South Australia has the quality of eternity, a moment that seems to be here forever. I have always liked the idea of time stopping. And here it happens. Often. In the subculture of the suburb beneath the city's notice.

The summer days are very long, often still. Sometimes you hear the wind in the trees and it sounds like rain, and you imagine the silent bliss of water falling through the sky.

Are people just temporary visitors on the earth? Are humans here forever? Or are we endangered, like soon-to-be-extinct birds under glass bell jars in museums, frisking up our collars of coloured feathers, standing still in our iridescent plumage, staring through windows at the distance?

In Oxford, in the Museum of Natural History at the top of the stairs, a large looming case of stuffed birds was almost hiding, a sample of murders and resurrections from all over the world perched on branches, wonder and pity in their glassy eyes.

Built in 1860, the neo-Gothic Museum, the design of which is inspired by John Ruskin's ideas about the importance of natural structures, is a large open court with multiple slender metal columns topped by cut metal botanic decorations holding up a vast glass tile and iron roof. The court is divided into five great galleries: one for mammals and birds; one for marine

NOVEMBER – the dodo and the dappled garden

creatures, amphibians and reptiles; one a mixture of things; one for rocks and minerals; and one for dinosaurs and fossils. The construction of the building was funded by sales of Bibles.

All around the court is a balcony or mezzanine, the thirty columns of its cloistered arcades each made from a different British stone. Each column has carved corbels and capitals of plant forms spanning the botanical orders of the world, resulting in resonant combinations like green serpentine and irises, limestone and narcissus, red serpentine and Moreton Bay pine, gypsum and orchids, grey granite and palms. The mingled poetry and concreteness of them link the outdoors underfoot world of silent stones and plants to this soaring glass and metal architecture, which is partly reminiscent of the Crystal Palace in London, the Grand Palais in Paris, or any other great 19th-century exhibition building or railway station around the world, one of those turn-of-the-century marvels of engineering. They contain so much glass because they were built before electricity was tamed.

The greatest treasure of the Oxford Museum is a mummified dodo head and foot, collectively called The Oxford Dodo. The full dodo was originally in the collection of the 17th-century gardener and collector John Tradescant, who collected treasures in his house in London that he called The Ark. It opened in the 17th century as Musaeum Tradescantianum, the first museum for the public in England. He began his collecting when he was sent from England to the Low Countries in Europe to buy fruit trees.

Dodos, last seen alive in 1662, are of course bywords/poster birds/icons/emblems for extinction. The story of their brutal and heedless extermination is sadly not unusual in stories of other living creatures, especially in Australia.

As I write a masked plover calls through the night. *Eee eee eee.* Then silence.

Dodo skeletons in museum collections are mostly conglomerations of different birds or casts from various bones. Most of the bones come from one swamp, the Mare aux Songe (The Sea of Dreams) in Mauritius, where a crowd of dodos is believed to have died looking for water in a very dry season about 4000 years ago. The man who found them in 1865, George Clarke, a schoolteacher, was inspired to look there by a book called *The Dodo and its Kindred* published in 1848.

Recent research shows that the dodo was closely related to the pigeon family, in particular the Nicobar pigeon, a spectacular bird with fabulous curling dark-blue and metallic-green iridescent feathers. Just after learning this I made a visit to Adelaide Zoo on a hot summer day, a wandering exploration kind of visit without a map and without a plan – just to see what was happening and to feast my eyes on some animal co-habitants of the earth.

I know there are people who don't like zoos because they think they are like prisons. I think they are more like hotels really, or hospitals. Though it was very hot many families, children, tourists and couples were visiting the zoo. In a low-fenced bird enclosure was a large group of Nicobar pigeons, sitting together around a pool of water. Quite a few were perched right near the wire fence and looked really intensely and directly at me.

Actually almost all the animals and birds I saw on that day met my eyes, they seemed to not only notice me but recognise me, or so I felt. It made me think about Dr Dolittle, who could not go into a pet shop because all the animals would recognise him and call out to him to buy them and take them home to live with him. I acknowledged this feeling of connection and recognition by clicking my tongue to communicate that I was alive and aware that they are living beings who see me just as much as I see them.

NOVEMBER – the dodo and the dappled garden

In 2011, on my way to enter the Oxford Museum of Natural History, I came across *The Ghost Forest Project* on the lawn outside. It consists of ten huge rainforest stumps from West Africa collected by artist Angela Palmer. The Project is her response to rainforest logging, an attempt to raise people's awareness of what is felled every day. It is said that every four seconds of every day a tropical forest the size of a football pitch is destroyed, something very hard to imagine. The stumps demonstrate the tragic scale of the problem by giving people direct experience of the size of the trees that are cut down.

Bleached pale grey by the sun, spanning great diameters, and including a lot of tough-looking roots, the scale of the tree stumps was dwarfing, astonishing, exciting. It was like seeing great dead elephants or whales. You were allowed to touch them but not to climb upon them. Their scale, their deadness, their provenance, and the surprise of them in Oxford, a place of elaborate architecture thick with human heritage, made a strong impact. The trees of *The Ghost Forest Project* were alien to the place and yet familiar and easily recognisable as tree stumps. The size of them against the architecture seemed to suggest a correspondence between the two: tree as museum or home, museum as tree or growth.

The Ghost Forest Project is now permanently homed in Wales at the National Botanic Garden, Carmarthenshire. Before being in Oxford for two years it was shown in Trafalgar Square in London, and outside the Danish Parliament in Copenhagen during the UN's Climate Change Conference in December 2009. In the middle of a great city *The Ghost Forest* would have made a great statement, as simple as death and as profound.

It took me quickly to tears seeing these skeletons, these bones, like me so far from their home, only they had travelled there to personalise environmental disaster by their individuality. These trees, you can't help thinking, could have lived to be thousands of years old, though these particular trees were harvested ethically, well most of them. The information board said: 'The trees in *Ghost Forest* – most of which fell naturally in adverse weather conditions – come from the Suhuma forest reserve in Western Ghana, a selectively logged concession run by John Bitar and Co, one of the largest timber producers in Ghana. They operate under strict licence from the Ghana Forestry Commission and run a Chain of Custody tracking system.'

Each tree was on a plain concrete plinth, which also held a plaque with information about what the wood from that particular tree is commonly used for and a diagram showing how big it would have grown had it stayed in the ground. The largest stump is 300 years old and weighs nineteen tons. Like zoo animals they are specimens of a larger story, a long way from home. They speak of the forest with immensely poignant voices. There was the Denya, the Wawa, the Danta, the Mahogany Dubini, the Dahoma, three types of Celtis, and the Anokye-Hyedua.

Four years earlier in Rome I had sought out the painted garden of the villa of the Empress Livia, wife of the Emperor Augustus. I stayed at the Hotel Oceania in Via Firenze, where the breakfast pastries and ham were truly marvellous. Tired after my long flight, lying on the double bed in my snug room tucked between the breakfast room and my ensuite, I read *Changing*, a 1977 autobiography from their library by Norwegian actor and lover of Ingmar Bergman, Liv Ullman.

The people in the hotel had never heard of Livia's painted garden but I found out where it was, ten minutes down the road in Palazzo Massimo, right near the Termini, the main train

NOVEMBER – the dodo and the dappled garden

station of Rome where I had to go to book my train ticket to Florence and which I was warned to avoid after dark.

The painted garden of Livia was first constructed in 30–20 BCE as a partly underground vaulted dining room, a cool place to eat and relax in summer. It was rediscovered and excavated in 1863 and moved to the museum in 1955 from Livia's suburban villa, fifteen kilometres north of Rome. The frescoes are said to be the most ancient example of continuous garden painting.

I know that I am drawn to wall painting not as illusionistic or *trompe l'oeil* works but as presence, as painting joined to architecture by a couple of persistent memories. One, my childhood visit to Pompeii and sighting of its roofless houses with their frescoed walls, lodged a dream world of ruins, colour and abraded surfaces in me. The other is the elegant stylised Japanese tree wallpapered on the wall of a childhood friend's parents' living room at Beaumont. Is it because the paintings bring the outside within? Is it because a wall is so flat and smooth and can so easily be touched? Is it too an echo of the shadows of gumtrees in my first home in the bush?

In the rest of the Palazzo Massimo museum there are fragments of the past, limbs of statues, sections of mosaics of squid, sea urchins and other creatures, a bust of Sappho looking like Jane Austen with curls in front of her ears and one of the strong face of Livia herself. She lived to be eighty-seven, was a wife, mother, grandmother, and a powerful individual who was deified in 42 AD by the emperor Claudius. She was the third wife of the emperor Augustus in a fifty-year marriage, mother of the emperor Tiberius, grandmother of the emperor Claudius, great-grandmother of the emperor Caligula, and great-great-grandmother of the emperor Nero.

Pliny's *Natural History* records the legend that on the day

153

of Livia's marriage to Augustus an eagle flew over the garden of her villa and dropped its dinner into her lap: a white chicken holding a branch of laurel in its beak. Livia rescued the chicken, and planted the laurel. The lone fowl inspired a chicken farm (the villa's nickname was *Ad Gallinas Albas* 'the white hens') and the laurel a grove of trees whose branches crowned the heads of triumphant Roman generals. Livia is said to have made the garlands.

In the wall painting twenty-four plant species are represented: the strawberry tree, bay laurel, oleander, holm oak, English oak, Cornelian cherry, myrtle, harts-tongue fern, early dog violet, crown daisy, chamomile, Italian cypress, quince, stone pine, pomegranate, opium poppy, cabbage rose, and date palm. There are lots of birds too, perching, exchanging information, washing, eating, flying, looking at one another or at the viewer.

The look of the garden fresco, mostly chalky blue and green with some red, yellow and brown, with its recognisable trees, shrubs and flowers all flowering and fruiting at once, creates an environment that does not imitate reality but celebrates the idea of a garden as a sanctuary promising eternity. And somehow the wind is there too.

It resembles my inherited garden and I am not sure if that is deliberate or it simply happened, if this is just what peaceful fruitful gardens are like in a Mediterranean climate. I too have a birdbath, and pigeons, piping shrikes, rosellas and other birds come to enjoy it. Today a pair of New Holland honeyeaters is visiting.

Often it seems that it really is Livia's garden out there through my window, the birds acting exactly like they do in her wall garden. Pigeons strut and look at each other or at me, others bathe or drink. I observe all the birds and their interactions as quietly as I can and with great joy. They wash noisily and often.

Sometimes when it is hot they just stand in the water soaking their feet. They drink long sips of water, and when they leave they do it in complete silence, except for the crested pigeons who make a squeaking noise when they fly.

And there is a hidden bird that repeatedly cries from the tree in the street outside our house. It says a few things often, which I try to interpret.

'The front bar is closed.'

'You can't do it all.'

'Second-hand clothes.'

'The world's cold.'

'Nothing to lose.'

It has a final judgement tone about it. An end of the evening comment. You can't argue.

One of the things I do when walking the dog is to ask other people the names of their dogs and then write them down on the blackboard painted on the kitchen wall when I get home, ostensibly to entertain my son. I am certain that one of the functions of dogs is to be clowns, to make people smile, with them, at them, around them. The dog names tend to back this up; reading the list is enough to make me smile most days, even though I read it often.

DECEMBER
words for home

The kitchen was always a great place to dance.
Patrick White

If it isn't happiness you can hang onto, it could be a broken garden pot, possibly worth mending, or the state of the cumquat tree.
Sylvia Lawson

Walking past the front of my house I see a place that looks as if a very old person is living in it. Someone whose roots have descended deep into this piece of land, this real estate, this temporary home. Where is the structure in the garden? Is it even a garden – maybe it is really a river, or a hillside? A bit of house painting is needed, the plants are not regulated but sprawl, it is clear they have not grown overnight or been planted as mature specimens but have been growing old in place. Here it would be easy to get lost and not mind.

And sometimes I feel like a character from a Patrick White novel and when out walking I see other characters – mid-morning or mid-afternoon they are standing in their gardens in their nightgowns. Not gardening, not reading, just standing, listening. They are hoping to not be seen but perhaps noticed. The White characters I might resemble are not the catty ones but the ones who stand, breathing, at the door.

Wherever I go in the world I see doppelgängers for dead writers and artists. Patrick White was playing tambourine in a whirling dervish band in Istanbul last time I saw him. Louise Bourgeois sits outside the pub smoking. W.G. Sebald often walks out of talks or is seen leaving a supermarket with a plastic bag. Rosalie Gascoigne is studying plants in the nursery. John Berger has a dog. Frida Kahlo is off to the football. Solitary and turned inwards Ian Fairweather is painting a house.

I only met one of my grandfathers and only a few times. The first time he was about eighty, blind and deaf. It is daunting to be told that someone has such disabilities. Yet earlier in our lives, when I lived on the other side of the world from him, we wrote a little to each other. In a fragile letter I wrote that he saved in a file I call myself 'your little flower' (*deine kleine Blume*) in German accompanied with, of course, a drawing of a flower, so something was going on between us.

I am retrospectively impressed by me as a young child writing a letter in German, my second language, trying to communicate, to be friendly, to connect with my grandfather. When we met in Melbourne he wanted me to sit on his knee but as I could see how frail that knee was I held my weight on my bent legs, which then got all trembly from the strain. I have never forgotten that. In a photo taken at the time he is bald with a spotty brown head, bent over and delicate, I am as pale as snow with curious dark almost black eyes, and a quiet listening protective look about me.

My paternal grandparents, Fritz and Gertrud, were called 'Rajah' and 'Ranee' because they honeymooned in Africa. I think of these words as typical names for elephants. They are Sanskrit words meaning great king and great queen, abbreviated from Maharajah and Maharanee. These words from India were somehow transposed to Africa thence to East Prussia, the US and finally Melbourne.

Their house on Whitehorse Road in Mitcham in Melbourne was dark, close and full of the scent of spices, something like gingerbread, chocolate, cloves, coffee and marzipan mixed together. There was also always a whiff of camphor. On the round wooden table was a cloth on which the names of visitors were signed and then embroidered in red thread. I have this cloth here folded up in a cupboard. It is made from very fine unbleached linen with a faded red border stitched on and a great stain across it, probably coffee. In the centre inside two concentric circles is embroidered *Haus Radok 1913*. Among the many signatures, some of which are very faded, is my father's, my mother's, my sister's and mine, possibly among the most recent additions as the red is quite bright. Rajah and Ranee were married in 1913 in Koenigsberg in East Prussia, so the tablecloth was started when they began life together. They had five children in the next eight years.

In 1938 Rajah lost his job at the Steinfurt Railway Stock Building Company in East Prussia because he was Jewish and so began to plan emigration. Many others had seen the Nazi writing on the wall and left much earlier. Three of his sons, including my father who was only eighteen, were in England. As Rajah had been in the German army and briefly served at the Russian front in Poland in World War One he was very reluctant to believe that he had to leave his prosperous life, his home, his job, his country. But at the outbreak of World War Two in 1939 he was arrested and imprisoned and his non-Jewish wife Ranee had to work hard to get him out, find funds, get accepted by another country, and get passports and visas for him, herself and their only daughter Gundula. He was arrested again in Genoa before the three of them finally arrived at Ellis

Island in February 1941. They found menial jobs in the US and eventually joined three of their sons in Australia in 1947.

I recall being especially interested in the exoticism of my grandparents, their names, their famous year-long honeymoon in Africa and what they brought back from it – among other things an elephant-foot bin, which I imagined but never got to see and a pet monkey called August. My persistent curiosity and questioning – or nagging – was eventually rewarded by the gift of three stiff black hairs from an elephant's tail plaited together.

Now I remember that Rajah visited us in Adelaide after Ranee died and bought a rosebush for us, called Superstar. He said it was the most beautiful rose in the world and it flowers still, but to me its salmon-orange colour is too bright. Another thing I recall was that he wanted to eat quark, a soft fresh cheese made from sour milk, for breakfast. To get it we had the great adventure of going into the Central Market with all its colour, crowds and delicious scents. It was a place my mother rarely went.

My paternal grandparents did not leave their substantial home in Koenigsberg with just a rucksack. In fact they left with twenty large trunks and fifteen pieces of hand luggage. Somewhere there is a long and curious list of what they took with them, or rather what Rajah took as the Jewish member of the household who had to list his belongings. It was mostly suits, shirts and shoes but also a typewriter, a stapler and staples, nine silver teaspoons, twelve silver coffee spoons and an amber paperweight.

When I met her, my grandmother Ranee was tall, thin and very tanned. She smoked incessantly using a long amber cigarette holder and always seemed to be wearing a long dark amber necklace and a sleeveless light amber-coloured dress, out of which wound her thin brown and intensely wrinkled arms.

Amber, fossil resin, the petrified sap of trees, is the semi-precious stone of the Baltic Sea. The best amber was found near Koenigsberg, collected on the beach. Amber was always present in our home. We were shown how to rub a lump of it to charge it with static electricity and pick up small torn pieces of paper.

My father grew up in East Prussia, the region on the Baltic Sea squeezed between Poland and Lithuania known for its lagoons and sand dunes. The city of Koenigsberg, now the Russian city of Kaliningrad, sits between two great north-facing lagoons. The few old German books that I have about that obscure now non-existent country are full of matte black-and-white photographs and stories telling the vivid history of its extinct tree-worshipping indigenous people and their animistic sculptures.

East Prussia is an obscure place but at any time may turn up. For example, just yesterday I read about it in Michel Tournier's autobiography *The Wind Spirit* where he describes it as having 'the vague boundaries of a mythical land with its Teutonic Knights, Porteglaives, and shifting dunes covered with swarms of migrant birds and a fantastic array of animals, including the auroch, or European bison, the wolf and the black swan'.

Then there are the more urbane stories about the scholar, philosopher, aesthetician and archetypal definer of the sublime Immanuel Kant taking his regular after-lunch walks through the city. There is the classic logic puzzle The Seven Bridges of Koenigsberg, the legend of the Amber Room, hideous accounts of the city's brutal sacking by the Russians at the end of World War Two, the subsequent erasure of the German presence there and its current situation as a Russian enclave, at present the only Russian city with a port that does not freeze over in winter.

East of Koenigsberg is the fishing village of Nidden, a place my father always yearned to return to. In the early 20th century it was visited by German expressionist painters like Max Pechstein, Karl Schmidt-Rottluff and Ernst Ludwig Kirchner who were interested in the dune landscape and the lagoons. Here the tallest sand dunes in Europe are found as well as the legendary High Dune and the Valley of Silence formed by wandering dunes. All the grainy black-and-white photographs of this place and its near environment, whether by various photographers or my father who did manage to visit there in 1965 and walk around his childhood sites, show an obsession with sand dunes from every possible close or distant angle. And with forests, flowers and the occasional elk.

It is or was a stark weather-observing kind of landscape, of wild simplicity and bareness. 'Oh look, how amazing!' the photographs seem to show the people saying to each other of the place that surrounds them, 'a shadow! a series of ridges on the dune! a few grasses silhouetted against the sky!'

This sense of spareness must be emblematic of the emotional experience of the place. There is not much to see but there is space and you feel it as much as see it. There is no accounting for the starkness of home. It might be the scent of honey, a white cup or a black bowl; it could be a tree or its shadow. Finding familiarity does not mean something intricate; it can as well be something almost empty. A certain texture of air can be what we call home. A house shapes the air in a certain way but then so does a tree, the sea, a flower or a cloud.

Because of the location of my father's birthplace in Koenigsberg and the regular holidays the family took in Nidden, once he was living in South Australia he was drawn to Kangaroo Island and the Coorong, the long lagoon stretching many kilometres along the South Australian coastline. In other words, to wild places full of sea air. And as he was an oceanographer he established research stations in both places.

I began a body of work in the year my father died but before he was ill by making drawings and taking photos at Cape Jervis, 100 kilometres south of Adelaide. The dog came with me and ran around there among the giant weeds next to the sea. I have a photo of him looking in the car door with a huge smile on his face. Looking from the Cape to the horizon you can see Kangaroo Island, known to the Ngarrindjeri people and other local tribes as Karta, the Island of the Dead. At some point in time the island was inhabited by Aboriginal people and then, about 2500 years ago, uninhabited when the water rose between the island and the mainland. In later years whalers and sealers lived there and took local and Tasmanian Aboriginal women to live with them, but that is another story.

Looking the long way over the sea to the island stirs something in me, releases something. How to explain that sensation of letting go or unloosening? It is a feeling like undoing your belt, but the one around your emotions or thoughts, not your waist. It's a letting go and knowing you are and going with it. Bob Marley sings about redemption songs, songs of freedom, and that is more like it. Your eyes travel, they see distance like a mirage but it is also palpable and present, and in the heart-expanding space between you seem able to fly.

The paintings that I made on raw, unprimed, unstretched canvas use the push-pull combination of describing both deep untouchable space and close haptic texture to send you both away and back, distant and up close. To let you simultaneously feel expansion and intimacy. And to thereby shift something in your body, to undo your belt. Almost like paintings for stage sets or indeed murals they are large and take up a good bit of wall. Each shows land and water, distance and proximity, in chalky blues and greens, with touches of yellow orange in the skies, on the sea or the edge of the clouds. Each painting involves masses of white. Its luminosity is like light shimmering on the sea.

Before painting the sky, the sea and the land I paint words on the back. Because the canvas is unprimed the paint strikes through the fabric and appears on the other side, but back-to-front and in a random way. This establishes a rough quality to the surface, which is then full of accidental effects such as you might see on an eroded gully or the rusted scrapes on an old metal truck you see beside you at the traffic lights. It speaks to you but not of skill or deliberation but of weather and movement, like clouds or lightning. The writing on the canvas is hidden inside the work. It is not visible except as an echo, a suggestion of pattern.

I made six such paintings for my exhibition called *Brightness falls from the air*, a line from a poem written by Thomas Nashe in 1593 about death and the Black Plague. The work was begun before it happened but ultimately had something to do with being by my father's bed when he was dying when the words of that poem, and others, such as Shakespeare's song 'Fear no more the heat of the sun' came into my head. And also, quite strongly and simply, the words *Day of Atonement*. And the Bob Dylan song 'Knocking on Heaven's Door'. And what did I do? I silently asked him to let go of life and sprayed perfume on a piece of paper, which I held under his nose. Though unconscious he sniffed strongly a few times and I am sure he got pleasure from that scent of something lovely in his last moments.

For me the brightness falling from the air was the subtle, rare, astonishing-yet-ordinary experience of death. But also a renewed sense of the vitality of the colour of the orange-yellow paint called Australian sienna like sunlight, and of light flickering on water. In the distance water frequently appears white. This is seen in mirages, in lakes, at the edge of the sea, as a *Silberstreife am Horizon*. Salt lakes are often a dissolving kind of pink but there is some suggestion of their expansiveness in the paintings too. To know brightness has fallen is also to know brightness.

Overall the paintings have more desire than skill in them, more longing than craft, more aspiration than achievement. Yet they are haunting and mesmerising, and their scale makes them enveloping. The experience of living with them pinned on the walls of our house has been remarkable. Each one is a giant window on a sublime place. They both transport and centre us.

Something in me fights against craftsmanship, I don't know what it is. If these paintings were expert *trompe l'oeil* works they would seem slick and facile to me, pre-digested rather than suggesting spaces in which to think, to breathe, to experience reverie and find the known in the unknown rough intersections of colour that snag your eyes. And like books the paintings have passages that you want to hold on to, to dogear, to return to. Maybe paintings have passages like houses, as a way of getting from one place to another?

Each painting in the *Brightness* series is called *Passage* and each has a subtitle both written in pencil and painted on its back: *this is where clouds are born; light green patches in the sea; Rapid Bay sea of light; clouds of birds over McLaren Vale; the rain came across the land invisible;* and *aaa eee iii ooo uuu.*

Also in the exhibition were a series of ten cast plaster books called *Collected Works of Goethe* and two large books called *Manual of Forgiveness (2 vols.)*. The Goethe books were cast from a hardback edition published in 1885 that my grandparents brought with them from East Prussia. It seemed a desecration to destroy such old books but they were unreadable because of their yellowed paper and old German typescript. To make something exquisite and enduring from their embossed covers was a way of giving them a longer life. In each cast I embedded fragments of mica I had collected in the Adelaide Hills. The mica gives each pink-tinted book an embodied treasure, a literally reflective surface. It is exquisitely shiny and enticing in broken silvery layers. Goethe, archetypal German *Dichter und Denker,* who was interested in plants, in colour, in minerals, in almost everything really, may well have liked them.

Manual of Forgiveness (2 vols.) was cast from two large de-accessioned library books from the University of South Australia, bound copies of some dry journal covered in thick red bookbinder's cloth and probably never opened. These cast books contain no mica and present faces of pinkish reddish surfaces, something like skin or fabric drawn thinly over the top of the plaster. One of them possesses a ghost shape like a page upon it where another book blocked the light thus changing the surface of the book and shifting its interaction with the plaster. These books connect strongly to my experience of my father, who was often difficult to be with and therefore needed a lot of forgiving. Such forgiveness was implicit and carried out in silence or in action rather than words. In this case it was imbued with a deep understanding of the impossible ambivalence of love that struck me forcefully at last as I witnessed him dying.

Because of its connection to the death of my father all the works in *Brightness falls from the air* involve an evocation and investigation of links between the northern and southern hemispheres, links that are cross-cultural, cross-geographical and cross-generational. They are present in one place and find another place in it. Would he have recognised something in them? I don't know. The experience of changing hemispheres involves seeing different stars yet also finding some familiarity.

As you move from Kaurna country to Ngarrindjeri country on the Fleurieu Peninsula there is a point where a different flavour enters the air. How to explain? All of Australia lives in a certain luminous light but there is some extra enchantment on the Fleurieu. You have to go there to experience it.

When I was a child there was no ball kicking, my family walked but not especially happily. Often we drove somewhere out of the city to be in a forest or climb hills to look at waterfalls. Once we walked to the mouth of the Murray River from Goolwa, a distance of ten kilometres. It was not fun — father striding in front, mother lingering at the back, sister complaining, me circulating as much as possible. The place is wild as can be, the strong roar of the open sea to one side filled with what my mother called 'white horses' and sand dunes to the other. The noisy windy white-flecked distance stretches out in front of you and as you trudge along with your nose full of salty air it seems that you are marching on the spot for all anything changes. On that walk I found a sailor doll that I still have. His hat says *Orcades*. Possibly but probably not a collector's item he sits on a bookshelf dressed in a blue velvet sailor suit with bright eyes, tight pink skin and just a little rip on his cheek.

We often went to Kuitpo Forest in autumn after it had rained to look for mushrooms under the pine trees. The slippery jacks we collected had shiny brown tops and dense yellow undersides. I could not eat them and suffered the anger of my father for this. He told me a story about an entire family dying from eating poisonous mushrooms, except for the one child who refused to eat them. The incentive to get me to eat them could only be, I suppose, my desire to not become an orphan.

A photograph taken around that time shows the two of us standing in front of our new Austrian tent. We put up this terribly modern, bright blue and orange pavilion with a floor and a window in the backyard in Adelaide. We could just stand up in it. I look happy though also like an orphan dressed in an old gingham dress and cardigan, my bare feet disappearing into the long grass. My father has a distant expression on his face; he seems to be thinking of something or someone elsewhere. When I see the old wooden fence behind us I remember now that there was once a black snake in this backyard, which my father killed with a spade before nailing its skin on the fence. Behind the house where there is now an oval was a retired dump when we moved in, full of hillocks of thick grass and piles of rubbish. It is said that most ovals in Adelaide began as rubbish dumps and that is why you find shards of old crockery at their edges.

There is another photograph of the two of us taken almost ten years later. We stand at the back of the garage squinting in the sun, again I am smiling, he is fierce. And not quite there. There is a tough smiling confidence in me and, in response, an expression of suspicion/challenge on his face.

A final photograph taken another ten years later, in Thailand, shows the two of us holding beers and looking at each other at an outdoor restaurant. We are both smiling and though there is still a sense of challenge and great levels of unknowability and incomprehension involved in our encounter I like to think there is a kind of resolution there. His blue eyes are finally in the place we are rather than somewhere else. And the beer is making our eyes shine.

The floor of the back veranda is grey concrete. Its metal roof is held up by three round metal posts, each of which lands in a circle of soil. Planted in one circle is an ornamental glory grapevine, which winds and twists up the pole and along the west and south sides. It has been there more than fifty years.

A wall of windows and a set of French doors face the veranda, which looks into a square of lawn and a walled garden in the centre of which is an apricot tree. Against the wall are an olive tree and a cypress. On the other side there are three compost bins. Beyond the oval and tennis courts over the back fence are houses and a creek along which big trees are growing. An arboretum was planted there in the 1850s so huge trees from eastern Australia, Queensland and the Mediterranean, and bamboo from China, wave their arms high in the air among the local giant manna, blue and river red gums.

On the veranda are an old pink formica and chrome table and four worn red plastic and chrome chairs, along with a large outdoor wooden table and a few white plastic chairs. There is a row of small chairs for children, collected as local heritage from hard rubbish days. There are several wooden yellow Schweppes crates evoking the art of Rosalie Gascoigne and holding saucers for plants and pots. There are piles of wood, a bag of BBQ charcoal, an old tin chest with bird-netting inside it, baseball bats and balls, a big empty ceramic jar from Bennett's Pottery, mosquito coils in a bowl and lanterns for candles. There is fertiliser in an old nappy bucket and a dragon tree in a pot.

This veranda has seen many dinners and long afternoons. It has heard many stories. It is an art studio, a refuge and a wonderful place to watch rain. When I sit there I feel that I belong. Sometimes the dog retreats there at night to look out for possums and stars, bats and owls. Always listening and looking he walks back inside the house slowly, not when called but when you demonstrate by standing still and looking that you too are interested in observing what is going on in the night. He is a thinker. Even in the day he will look at birds flying in the sky, stopping to watch them quietly and with attention.

DECEMBER – words for home

The silence of the dog is vast and immensely comforting. It is interspersed with nagging and fretting, significant breaths and occasional lip smacking. While he is silent I am asking questions and worrying at ideas. Sometimes I put words in his mouth so we can have a conversation. He can be consoling, cheeky, poetic and wise or even make jokes but not all the time as that can get wearing. You could be a bird I say to him, you could be one too, says he.

References

EPIGRAPHS

Arundhati Roy, *War Talk*, South End Press, 2003, p. 112.

January

Rosalie Gascoigne, 'there are only lovers and others: interview with Rosalie Gascoigne', Ewen McDonald, *Antic 8*, December, New Zealand, 1990.

February

John Updike, *Museums and Women and other stories*, first pub. 1973, Penguin, 1975, p. 17.

March

Louise Bourgeois, goodreads.com.

April

Andy Warhol and Pat Hackett, *Popism*, first pub. 1980, Penguin, 2007, p. 362.

May

Jeanette Winterson, 'A Gift of Wings', in *Art Objects: essays on ecstasy and effrontery*, Vintage, 1996, p. 71.

June

Joseph Beuys, *Jeder Mensch ist ein Künstler (Make the Secrets Productive)*, manifesto, 1977.

July

Agnès Varda, spoken in opening scene of *The Beaches of Agnès*, 2008.

August

Virginia Woolf, *A Room of One's Own*, first pub. 1928, Penguin, 1974, p. 105.

September

Michael Hamburger, 'An Essay on Essays', in *Art as Second Nature: Occasional Pieces*, Manchester, Carcanet New Press Ltd, 1975.

October

Vladimir Holan, 'Between': *Selected Poems*, Penguin Modern European Poets, trans. by Jarmila & Ian Milner, 1971, p. 102.

November

Apollinaire, 'The Pretty Red-head', *Selected Poems*, Penguin Modern European Poets, trans. by Oliver Bernard, Penguin, first pub. 1965, reprinted 1970, p. 52.

December

Patrick White, *Three Uneasy Pieces*, Pascoe Publishing, first pub. 1987, reprinted 1988, p. 15.

Sylvia Lawson, 'How Simone de Beauvoir died in Australia', in *How Simone de Beauvoir died in Australia: stories and essays*, UNSW Press, 2002, p. 188.

REFERENCES

QUOTES IN TEXT

PAGE 7
Hossein Valamanesh, exhibition catalogue, essay by Stephanie Radok, 'Fingers of memory', Sherman Galleries, 1999.

PAGE 30
Dorrit Black, letter to the editor, *Advertiser*, 27 April 1946, p. 12.

PAGE 32
Geoffrey Bardon and James Bardon, *Papunya: a Place made after the Story*, Miegunyah Press, 2004, p. 380.

PAGE 39
Philip Drew, *Veranda: Embracing Place,* Angus and Robertson, 1992, p. 103.

PAGE 60
Paul Lafargue, *The Right to be Lazy,* written Saint Pélagie Prison, 1883 (worth reading in full). https://theanarchistlibrary.org/library/paul-lafargue-the-right-to-be-lazy

PAGE 77
Rudolf Steiner, 4 June 1924, in *Joseph Beuys and Rudolf Steiner: Imagination Inspiration Intuition*, exhibition catalogue, National Gallery of Victoria, 2007, p. 32. Exhibition dates: 26 October 2007–17 February 2008.

PAGE 78
op. cit., Joseph Beuys, 21 October 1971, letter to Manfred Schradi, p. 88.

PAGE 80
https://en.wikipedia.org/wiki/How_to_Explain_Pictures_to_a_Dead_Hare

PAGE 88
Rosa Luxemburg, *Die russische Revolution Eine kritische Würdigung*, 1920, p. 109.

PAGE 88
Emma Goldman, *Living my Life,* Knopf, 1934, p. 56.

PAGE 89

Rosa Luxemburg, Prison Letter, 2 May 1917.
https://www.marxists.org/archive/luxemburg/1917/05/02.htm

PAGE 102

Abel Rodriguez https://www.documenta14.de/en/artists/13538/abel-rodriguez

Download his free book from: *https://www.tropenbos.org*

PAGE 107

Louis Riel, 4 July 1885. http://www.mmf.mb.ca/louis_riel_quotes.php

PAGE 123

Djambawa Marawili quoted by Will Stubbs in acceptance speech, 2015 Australia Council Visual Arts Board Award for Advocacy: https://blogs.crikey.com.au/northern/2015/03/19/art-land-and-people-will-stubbs-on-why-homelands-matter/

PAGE 123

Amanda Lohrey, 'The clear voice suddenly singing', in *Secrets*, 1997, Pan Macmillan, p. 268.

PAGE 124

op. cit., p. 257.

PAGE 140

'Emil Radok and the Taming of Demons', Spring 2003 issue of *Kinema*, Jin Vorac: https://openjournals.uwaterloo.ca/index.php/kinema/article/view/1048/1186

PAGE 160

Michel Tournier, *The Wind Spirit*, Beacon Press, trans. by Arthur Goldhammer, Collins, 1989, p. 90.

ACKNOWLEDGEMENT

I would like to acknowledge the usefulness of my father's website: http://mpec.sc.mahidol.ac.th/RADOK/page1.html

Index

A
Academus 25
Acosta, Pavel 120
Adelaide Festival, 1980, 27; 1996, 2
Alcoze, Thomas 52
Alexander the Great 45
Alice Springs/Mparntwe 9
Anthroposophical Museum 78
Arachne 25
Araluen Valley 57
Athena 25

B
Bardon, Geoffrey and James *Papunya: a Place made after the Story* 32
Bashkirtseff, Marie 71
Becher, Bernd and Hilla 38
Bellini, Giovanni *The Ecstasy of Saint Francis* 90
Beltram, Ramon Miranda 120
Berger, John 157
Beuys, Joseph: *Untitled (Bumerang mit Spiegel)* 68; *ja, ja, ja, ja, ja, nee, nee, nee, nee, nee* 75; *Richtkräfte (Einer neuen Gesellschaft)* 75 ; *Silberstreife am Horizon* 78; How to explain art to a Dead Hare 80; *Umschlitt (Tallow)* 81; *Das Ende des 20 Jahrhundert (The End of the 20th Century)* 81; *Intuition* 82

Biggers, Sanford 118
Black, Dorrit *The olive plantation* 29, 52
Black, J.M. 52
Boas, Franz 119
Bourgeois, Louise 157
Bradman, Donald 110
Briceño, Antonio *Gods of America* 67
Bronzino, Agnolo *Venus, Cupid, Folly and Time* 34
Broulee 53
Burrunkuy 11

C
Canadian Museum of Civilisation, Gatineau 104
Captains Flat 50
Cardiff, Janet *The Forty Part Motet* 122
Carr, Emily 100-102
Castor and Pollux 25
Ch'eng T'ang 96
Chicago, Judy *The Dinner Party* 117
David Chipperfield Architects 41
Claxton, Dana *Buffalo Bone China* 103
The Cloisters, Fort Tryon Park 121
Clarke, Marcus 55
Constantinople 2
Coorong 161

Cotton Genesis 2
Cribb A.B. and J.W. *Wild Food in Australia* 55
Crystal Palace, London 26, 149
Czech Museum of Ethnography, Prague 135

D

Danko, Aleks, Joan Grounds, David Lourie, David Stewart, *We should call it a living room* 115
Davenport, Samuel 26
Dharug 68
documenta 60
Dr Dolittle 150
Dong, Song *Doing Nothing Garden* 60
Drew, Philip 39
HMT *Dunera* 87
Dürer, Albrecht *Selbstbildnis mit Eryngium (Self-portrait with thistle)* 49; *The Great Piece of Turf (Das große Rasenstück)* 60
Dylan, Bob *Knocking on Heaven's Door* 163

E

Egyptian Room, South Australian Museum 42
Eliot, T.S. *The Waste Land* 92; *Preludes* 93
Ennigaldi 30
Eno, Brian *Thursday Afternoon* 98; *Mistaken Memories of Medieval Manhattan* 112
Erindale 109

F

Fairweather, Ian 157
Fawlty Towers 78
Fenellosa, Ernest 94
Fitzgerald, F. Scott *The Great Gatsby* 126
Frick Museum, New York 89

G

Galen 45
Gascoigne, Rosalie 157, 168
Museum für Gegenwart, Hamburger Bahnhof, Berlin 58, 81
Gethsemane 28
Ginsberg, Allen 126
von Goethe, Johann Wolfgang 50, 164
van Gogh, Vincent 102
Goldman, Emma 88
Gonzalez-Lang, Ignacio 120
The Goon Show 51
Gough, Julie 52

H

Hall, Dorothy 55
Havel, Vaclav 140
George Gustav Heye Centre, New York 124
Hermannsburg/Ntaria 10
Høeg, Peter *A History of Danish Dreams* 66
Höfer, Candida 40
Homer 31
Humann, Carl 44
Humboldt Forum 24

Index

J
Jackson, A.Y. 100

K
Kakadu National Park 10
Kahlo, Frida 43, 157
Kaliningrad 160
Kampa Museum, Prague 136
Kangaroo Island 72, 161
Kaurna 109, 110, 165
Kiefer, Anselm 37
Knight, John *The Right to be Lazy* 58
Koenigsberg 132, 158
Kolář, Viktor 133
Koloděje nad Lužnicí 138
Kreckler, Derek 34
Krížek, Jan 134
Kubrick, Stanley *Clockwork Orange* 139
Kynaston, Edward *The Penguin Book of the Bush* 55

L
Lafargue, Paul *The Right to be Lazy* 59
Laterna Magika 140
Lebrecht, Franz 87
Lessing, Gotthold Ephraim 59
Leunig, Michael 55
Li Bai/Li Po 94
Empress Livia 152
Lohrey, Amanda 123
Lozano-Hemmer, Rafael *Pulse Room/Almacén de Corazonadas* 44
Luxemburg, Rosa 88

M
Malouf, David *The Great World* 66
Marawili, Djambawa 123
Mare aux Songe/The Sea of Dreams 150
de Maria, Walter *The Earth Room* 114
Marquez, Gabriel Garcia *One Hundred Years of Solitude* 65
Mead, Margaret 120
MONA Museum of Old and New Art, Hobart 44, 93
Monty Python 34
Mouseion 31, 135
Mount of Olives 28
Mucha, Alphonse 130

N
Namatjira, Albert 10
Náprstek Museum of Asian, African and American Cultures, Prague 136
National Gallery of Art, Ottawa 99
National Gallery of Australia, Canberra 78
National Gallery of Victoria, Melbourne 75
Nauman, Bruce *No no no museum* 74; *The true artist helps the world by revealing mystic truths* 82
Nebuchadnezzar 46
Nefertiti 41, 43
Ngarrindjeri 162
Nidden 160
Noah, William 102
Novalis 77

O

Oberlander, Cornelia Hahn 99
O'Keefe, Georgia 102
Orpheus 31
Oxford Museum of Natural History 22, 148

P

Pacific Cultures Gallery, South Australian Museum 42
Palazzo Massimo, Rome 152
Palmer, Angela *The Ghost Forest Project* 151
Papunya Tula 7, 32, 118
Pausanias 30
Pergamon Museum 34
Phasmid Studios, Berlin 35
Phoenix, Frances 117
Pitt Rivers Museum, Oxford 22
Plato 25
Pode Bal 131
Pootoogook, Annie 102
Pootoogook, Itee 102
Pound, Ezra *Cathay* 94; *Epitaphs* 95; *The Pisan Cantos* 96; *The Exile's Letter* 97
de Predis, Giovanni Ambrogio *Portrait of a Lady* 16
Preston, Margaret 101
Prometheus 25

Q

Quadriga 4
Qureshi, Imran 112

R

Radok, Alfred *The Long Journey (Daleká cesta)* 138
Radok, David 131
Radok, Emil (Elias) 132
Radok, Stephanie *The Immigrant's Garden* 2; *The Weight of Words* 42; *The Province is Ideal for Art* 7; *in the beginning was the world* 51; *weedmaps* 54; *Lost Books* 72; *what we bring with us* 87; *Brightness falls from the air* 163; *Manual of Forgiveness (2 vols.)* 164
Rakowitz, Michael *The Invisible Enemy Should Not Exist* 47
Reid, Bill *The Spirit of Haida Gwaii* 105
Martin Řezníček, *Jan Křížek, Sculpture and Bees* 134
Riel, Louis 107
Ringwood 14
Rodriguez, Abel *Seasonal Changes in the Amazon Forest* 102

S

Saint Francis 90
Sakahàn 102
Schliemann, Heinrich 30
Schneider, Marius 123
Sebald, W.G. 157
Shakespeare and Sons, Prague 129
Steiner, Rudolf 75
Stendhal syndrome 35
Struth, Thomas 38

Sydney Biennale, 1979, *European Dialogue* 39; 1982, *Vision in Disbelief* 112

T
Taiga Garden, Ottawa 99
Theresienstadt/Terezín 139
Tomatis, Albert 123
Topkapi Palace 64
Tournier, Michel *The Wind Spirit* 160
Tradescant, John 149
Tropenbos 102
Troy 30
Tjungurrayi , Yala Yala Gibbs 118

U
Ur 30

V
Valamanesh, Hossein 7, *Dwelling* 27
Veletrzni Palace, Prague 129
da Vinci, Leonardo *Madonna of the Rocks* 16
Võ, Danh *We the People* 46
Vonnegut, Kurt 57

W
Waterlow, Nick 39
Welles, Orson *Citizen Kane* 139
White, Patrick 157
Wilson, Fred *Blossom* 118
Wölfli, Adolf *Christopher Columbus* 134

X
Xiao, Zhu *Jiuhuang bencao / Famine relief herbal* 55

Wakefield Press is an independent publishing and
distribution company based in Adelaide, South Australia.
We love good stories and publish beautiful books.
To see our full range of books, please visit our website at
www.wakefieldpress.com.au
where all titles are available for purchase.
To keep up with our latest releases, news and events,
subscribe to our monthly newsletter.

Find us!

Facebook: www.facebook.com/wakefield.press
Twitter: www.twitter.com/wakefieldpress
Instagram: www.instagram.com/wakefieldpress

www.ingramcontent.com/pod-product-compliance
Lightning Source LLC
Chambersburg PA
CBHW071023240526
45469CB00006BD/2069